MISSING PIECES

A FAMILY STORY RETOLD

MISSING PIECES

A FAMILY STORY RETOLD

M. David Isaak and Beth Gerson

Photograph in the authors' private collection

© 2020 M. David Isaak, Beth Gerson
Published by GERISA INC. All Rights Reserved.
https://www.gerisabooks.org

Missing Pieces: A Family Story Retold

No part of this publication may be reproduced, stored in a retrieval system or transmitted in any form or by any means, electronic, mechanical, photocopying, recording, or otherwise without written permission of the authors.

Although every precaution has been taken to verify the accuracy of the information contained herein, the authors and publisher assume no responsibility for any errors or omissions. No liability is assumed for damages that may result from the use of information contained within.

Hardcover ISBN: 978-1-7353296-1-1
Softcover ISBN: 978-1-7353296-0-4

Library of Congress Control Number:
2020912828

Includes bibliographical and historical references
and a chronological guide to the correspondence.

Printed in the United States of America
First Edition 2020

Translations and book design by M. David Isaak

The cover photographs, translations and photographs of the correspondence are in the authors' private collection. Attributions for all other photographs are provided throughout this volume.

"I remember it well," she murmured...

"The day was Wednesday, November 9, 1938. We had taken the train from Berlin to Leipzig, where we thought it would be safer. When the train arrived, we peered out the window and saw Nazi Storm Troopers everywhere. We were so afraid. We crouched down in the train, not making a sound, and remained there until morning..."

I did not dare interrupt her story for fear of missing a word.

Our Story: Martha & Pinkas Isaak, GERISA INC, 2020.

MISSING PIECES

CONTENTS

ACKNOWLEDGMENTS	9
PROLOGUE	11
PART 1	15
Galicia to Germany	15
Exclusion and Elimination of Jews	16
The Pre-War Years	17
The Rise of Adolf Hitler	18
PART 2	27
The *Polenaktion*	28
Operation Barbarossa / *Einsatzgruppen*	29
Sigmund and Josef Weinreb	30
Leopold Weinreb	32
Noah Weinreb	34
Pinkas Isaak	35
Resilience and Rebuilding	36
PART 3	39
Guide to the Correspondence	39
Letters and Postcards	83
EPILOGUE	85
Annotations and Endnotes	87

MISSING PIECES

ACKNOWLEDGMENTS

Missing Pieces: A Family Story Retold is dedicated to the stories of aunts, uncles and grandparents who have been long missing from our family narrative, expressed in their words in real time. We are grateful to surviving family members for sharing their recollections and to all those whose scholarship has added significantly to our understanding of historical events. Their knowledge and insights have enabled us to create a strong framework for the correspondence.

Care has been given to translating the correspondence with authenticity and providing context with historical accuracy. Sources include first person accounts and records archived in The Central Database of Shoah Victims' Names at Yad Vashem, the United States Holocaust Memorial Museum, the *Memorial Book–Victims of the Persecution of Jews under the National Socialist Tyranny in Germany 1933-1945* in the German Federal Archives (*Das Bundesarchiv*), the YIVO Institute for Jewish Research, the Museum of Jewish Heritage–A Living Memorial to the Holocaust, the Jewish Museum Frankfurt, the Jewish Museum Berlin, JewishGen, and the American Jewish Joint Distribution Committee.

Specific references and resources are cited in the Annotations and Endnotes at the end of this volume.[1]

MISSING PIECES

PROLOGUE
New York City, 2020

As a child, the word "Holocaust" was not in my vocabulary, much less when used as a term defining 12 years that forever changed the lives of so many families, including mine. Like many offspring of parents who lost family members during the Holocaust, I knew little about the early lives of even my closest relatives and virtually nothing about those who were no longer with us.

My parents were born and raised in Germany. While I knew little about their childhood experiences and family history, I was aware from an early age of the importance they placed on maintaining close ties with family members who were scattered across three continents after the war. Throughout nearly 70 years of marriage, my parents always looked forward with great anticipation to visits with family living near and far. I have come to understand their guarded references long ago to "The Family"—a family that no longer included their fathers and siblings who were lost in Europe from 1938 through 1945.

I was born in Wales in 1939, the only child of parents who had escaped Berlin only months before. My earliest memories were of wartime London: spending nights in the Underground for safety and coming back to the street at daybreak to see if our building had been bombed; sitting on my father's shoulders in Trafalgar Square on the evening of May 8, 1945, as the lights were turned on for the first time in more than five years and the crowd cheered. The war was over and my immediate world felt all the more safe. I would not know for many years to come that so many family members were gone or the details of their passing.

In 1949, we moved to Israel. From the window of our one-room flat in Tel Aviv, I was able to look out and see donkeys pulling their loads over the sandy street below and the harbor where my father and I went swimming during those early days of the newly created State of Israel. The remains of a ship stood where it had run aground nearby. My cousin Alex said it was called the "Altalena." Seventy years later, I would come to know the story of that ship and its connection to the Irgun *(Irgun Ze'vai Le'umi)*, the organization my Uncle Leopold joined in Palestine after leaving Berlin in 1934.[2] He likely fought with an associated organization during the Warsaw ghetto uprising nine years later.[3]

In 1953, soon after my bar mitzvah, my parents announced that we were moving to America. We sailed to England and boarded a second ship to the United States after a brief stop in

Bar Mitzvah of M. David (Moshe) Isaak
Tel Aviv, 1952
Photograph in the authors' private collection

London, where we watched the coronation of Queen Elizabeth II with family that had settled in England after the war. In America, my parents worked and I completed my education. I became a dentist, settled in New Jersey, and raised a family. In retirement, my parents moved to Florida, where they enjoyed the warm winters and their new community. They returned to New York in 2004.

Throughout those busy years, conversations occasionally turned to the war and family members who had not survived, but it was not until 1997 that my parents began to share their story. We were visiting the Museum of Jewish Heritage—A Living Memorial to the Holocaust in Manhattan. My mother stopped abruptly in front of an exhibit entitled "Kristallnacht" and began to recount the events of November 9, 1938, when she and my father had attempted to flee Berlin. She stood quietly for a time and then murmured, "I remember that night…" The expression on her face spoke volumes.

Since that visit to the Museum, Beth and I have studied the time period, traveled in the footsteps of those who came before us, and helped my parents write a book recording their memories of the tumultuous years marking the rise of the Nazi Party and their escape from

Germany. Their story and thus mine is intertwined with the stories of other family members, both those who survived and those who perished in the flames of hate nearly 80 years ago.

My father passed away in 2008. While helping my mother organize a lifetime of papers and books, we discovered a tattered brown envelope stuffed with letters and postcards written in German, Yiddish and Hebrew during the 1930s and 1940s. My Aunt Eva, who had married in 1937 and lived in Portugal throughout the war, was the recipient of the correspondence. It remained in her keeping for decades. Years later, her children sent the envelope to my parents and they brought it with them to New York. The cache of letters and cards in the faded envelope had remained remarkably intact.

During the years that followed, I translated the letters and cards into English, and the stories they held began to emerge. Gradually, Beth and I came to know what had happened to family members who were missing from my childhood: uncles, aunts, cousins, and grandfathers. Moreover, the correspondence has helped us to understand the incredibly difficult decisions each writer had to make under circumstances that were often beyond his or her control: whether to leave Germany during the years when leaving was still possible, join the Resistance, or share with an elderly mother the news of her son's death in a concentration camp.

After the war, surviving family members settled in England, America and what would become the State of Israel. While no longer living near one another, they continued to gather for occasions large and small. The first gathering was in London in 1946, in honor of my mother's cousin, Leo Margulies, upon his return from the Buchenwald concentration camp. A photograph taken that day can be found on page 37 of this volume.

Stories shared over the years have provided the framework for a narrative that now includes the voices of family members lost during the Holocaust. Throughout the writing process, we have been reminded at every turn that my grandfathers, aunts and uncles were unaware of what was happening beyond their own circumstances. It is our hope that *Missing Pieces: A Family Story Retold* will enrich our collective understanding of circumstances and events as they unfolded and compel us to seek answers to the many questions that remain.

MDI

MISSING PIECES

PART 1
Galicia to Germany

Alter Meier Isaak
1877 – Unknown

Mindl (Ehrenreich) Isaak
1877 – 1933

Photographs in the collection of
The Museum of Jewish Heritage—A Living Memorial to the Holocaust, New York, NY
Gift of Beth Gerson and M. David Isaak

Exclusion and Elimination of Jews

From the time Adolf Hitler came to power, a defining goal of the Nazi Party was the exclusion of Jews from all rights and protections. On September 15, 1935, the Nuremberg Laws (Reich Citizenship Law) stripped Jews of German citizenship by defining a citizen as "one of German or kindred blood."[4] The ideology in which the laws were grounded excluded all Jews from the rights given to Germans as defined by the law.

The families of Alter Meier Isaak and Noah Weinreb immigrated to Germany from Galicia, a province in what is now southeastern Poland, during a time of increasing antisemitism and limited financial opportunity for Jews in the region. Both men and their offspring held Polish passports. Their status as Polish nationals strongly affected the experiences and immediate fate of Alter Meier, Noah, and three of their sons in October 1938, when Nazi Germany expelled approximately 17,000 Polish nationals residing in the German Reich during the *Polenaktion* (Polish Action).[5]

Alter Meier Isaak was born in Tarnow, Galicia, in 1877. He married Mindl Ehrenreich, who was also from Galicia. The couple settled in Ludwigshafen am Rhein and later moved to Leipzig. They had eight children: Elias, Fannie, Sascha (Sali), Hulda (Hilda), Jonas, Bernhard, Pinkas and Josef. By the mid-1930s, only Pinkas, Sascha (Sali) and Hulda remained in Leipzig.[6] As a Polish national, Alter Meier was deported during the *Polenaktion* in October 1938.[7]

Sascha Isaak married Wilhelm Krausz, who was born in Lackenbach, Austria.[8] Thus, they were not affected by the *Polenaktion*. The couple lived in Leipzig and had a son named Ernst. Official records in the *Memorial Book–Victims of the Persecution of Jews under the National Socialist Tyranny in Germany 1933-1945* in the German Federal Archives (*Das Bundesarchiv*) state that all three were deported to the Riga ghetto on January 21, 1942. Wilhelm died in the Auschwitz III–Monowitz forced labor camp on September 29, 1944.[9]

Noah Weinreb, a son of Hinda and Abraham Weinreb, was born in Nowy Sącz, Galicia, in 1891. He served in the Austro-Hungarian Army. In 1913, the family moved to Germany. Noah married Ella Rottenberg, a daughter of Rabbi Moses and Rachel Rottenberg, who were both from Kurima, Hungary. Noah and Ella settled first in Nuremberg near Noah's family and later moved to Berlin. They had nine children: Eva, Leopold, Martha, Sophie, Sigmund, Josef, Jenny, Lazarus and Benno.

A FAMILY STORY RETOLD

The Pre-War Years
1933 – 1938

Antisemitic Poster
Berlin, Germany, 1930s
Photograph in the authors' private collection

"Bad Kissingen: Es war einmal…"
Translation: "Bad Kissingen: It was once…"

The poster portrays Jewish figures superimposed on the photograph of a German vacation spa. The man and woman standing together on the left are Rav Moshe Dovid Rottenberg and his wife Rochel. They are the author's great-grandparents.

17

The Rise of Adolf Hitler and the Third Reich[10]
"To Stay or to Go?"

Alter Meier Isaak and Noah Weinreb were observant Jews who had immigrated to Germany, established successful businesses, and were raising their families in relative peace and security. This was not to last. Peace and security for Jews in particular were short-lived in a post World War I Germany that was struggling under the weight of reparations, destruction, and a devastated national morale.

Under the leadership of Adolf Hitler, the National Socialist German Workers' (Nazi) Party made Jews the scapegoat for the country's ills and their destruction a solution that required complete allegiance to the man and party dedicated to restoring Germany to honor and glory. Hitler's ascent to power in January 1933 and the appointment of high party officials dedicated to his methods and goals made possible the implementation of policies focused on ostracizing and ultimately expunging the country of its Jews.

From 1933 through 1945, Joseph Goebbels, the Reich Minister of Propaganda, provided able oversight to a department that saturated all means of public communication with populist propaganda, proclaiming a clear message to a nation of comrades unified by race. From childhood, all men and women of Aryan descent were expected to dedicate themselves to party principles and a racial ideology grounded in a steady diet of hatred toward those unlike themselves. Earlier anti-Jewish sentiment was easily transformed into virulent antisemitism that demonized Jews and demanded adherence to policies that would lead to their annihilation, first in Germany and later throughout Europe.

Jewish families lived with daily uncertainty, persecution and increasing isolation. As it became clear that Nazi policies were becoming ever more draconian, Ella and Noah Weinreb were faced with nearly impossible decisions and few choices. Members of their extended family began to leave Germany, as would their eldest three children.

Among the first to leave Germany were Noah's parents and brothers, Adolf and Heinrich (*Yechezkel*), who immigrated to Palestine in 1933, followed in 1934 by Ella's sister Toni and her husband. That same year, Ella and Noah's 19-year-old son Leopold joined a Jewish youth movement and departed for Palestine as well. Given Leopold's age at the time and his later affiliation with the Irgun (*Irgun Ze'vai Le'umi*), it is likely that he joined Betar, an activist young adult movement.[11]

While teenagers Sigmund and Josef might have gone to Palestine on the Youth Aliyah program, that option was deferred. Daughters Eva and Martha also remained at home until they married in 1937 and 1938, respectively. Eva moved with her husband to Portugal, which remained neutral throughout the war. Martha and her husband Pinkas fled Germany in December 1938.

The three letters on pages 20-25 were written by Noah's brother in 1935 and 1937. They bring into sharp focus the dilemma faced by many Jewish families.

Ella Weinreb and Eva in front of the family's produce shop
Berlin, Germany

Photograph in the authors' private collection

MISSING PIECES

Yechezkel (Noah's brother) to niece Eva in Berlin
Kibbutz Ein Charod, Palestine, ca. 1935

Dear Eva! – *Shalom*.

A long time has elapsed since we have written each other, especially since I had no reason to write you. However the situation now requires a different approach, one in which one must not wait till the last minute, especially since "coming-to-the-Land" has now become more difficult, and you, Eva, must take note of this.

You consider your "home" responsibilities to be far more important than being able to come to Palestine. But now that the economic situation has become even more dire, THE solution is for you to move out of your home as quickly as possible. Without any planning such as *Hachshara*, or enrolling Martha, Sophie etc. in their "Youth-Aliyah" program, this dear family is just gathered, awaiting God's help; – and is doing nothing to help themselves.

Well, dear Eva, you have the urgent desire to come here, – I can understand that, but do you think that's right, even before you put Martha, Sophie, Sigmund and Joseph in "Youth-Aliyah?"

These four must first be here in the Land and settled, then you can come, but only you. Noah and Ella can not arrange the accommodation of these 4 "grown-ups" [teens] as readily as you could.

Had you followed my advice at the time, today you would be here, and you would have qualified to be able to bring in your parents. There was no easier and secure way.

So now, the "so-very-loving" family is shut in at home, with no backup plan or money, and thinks God will help, even if one waits and hopes till 120 years.

So now I'm taking the liberty to prepare you, dear Eva, that you, especially you, have to take care of the four first. You must set things in motion so that they will come to Palestine with the next Youth-Aliyah group. I am positioned here to undertake everything to deal with this and the difficulties associated with it. First the children must be housed here and then come the parents.

In this way you will start on the proper path that will also be a relief for your parents. But I confess to you, dear Eva, that I cannot take any steps on your behalf, as long as you have not provided for the four — they must be <u>in the Land</u>, and only then — —

Dear Evi, don't be angry at me, my darling, that I write you so forcefully, but it is THE most important step, and it must be taken. When I see the local youth groups here, how capable they have become, how they stand out, then I think so much about your "four"…

Dear Evi, hopefully now you understand me better and you'll act, undaunted and not resentful, because there's still time. Inform me what you have undertaken and I surely can do much to help you from here,. Sit down immediately and communicate with the specific organizations, initiate everything, because shortly *Chaver* [member] Ziesling from Ein Charod will come there — he is on the council of the Youth-Aliyah and can accomplish much for me.

Well, dear Evi, enclosed is a detailed letter with enclosures from which you'll understand that, for me, things are good and wonderful.

Shalom, **Yechezkel**

MISSING PIECES

Yechezkel to brother Noah in Berlin.
Kibbutz Ein Charod, Palestine, ca. 1937

Dear Brother Noah, Shalom! [untill 120]

When I received your letter, I immediately tried to do what I could, but I had to wait a long time to get an accurate opinion. Well, there is a solution, but there also are great difficulties that cannot be bypassed.

A valid application is accepted only from children whose parents are over 55 years old. The government (British Mandate) also requires proof that you can earn an additional 5 Pounds monthly for each person and that includes your dear children – how do you imagine doing that? When I mentioned that the children are grown-up and able to work, they pointed out that children 16, 17 and 18 years old, Youth-Aliyah age, are excluded.

If you call to mind what I wrote to you about two years ago, you will remember my thoughts about the urgency to act then, but unfortunately you, as well as Eva, did not follow my advice. Without completing the necessary steps, getting into this country is hopeless, and you cannot get an entry certificate – and [if you could] it would have to be with a Capital (cash) certificate.

I believe there's only one path you must take first: Martha, Sophie, Sigmund and Josef – enroll them in the Youth-Aliyah (program) and in some months they can make Aliyah.

22

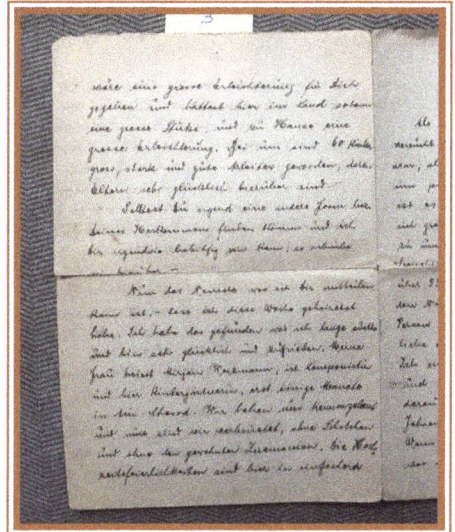 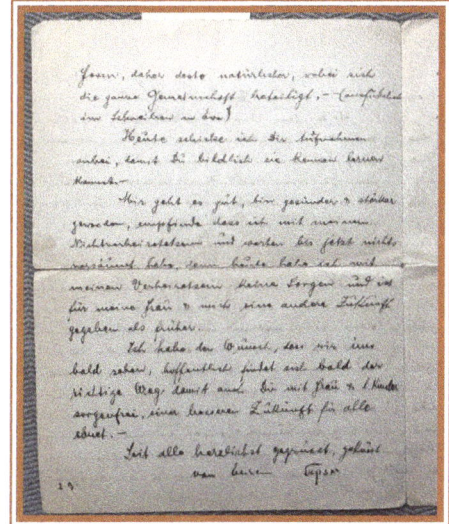

Sit yourself down immediately and communicate with Mordechai Shafua, Berlin-Meinickestrasse 10, "*Hechalutz*", he will take you by the hand and advise you of all the "ins and outs", since he is a *Chaver* [member] of Ein Charod and also manages these kind of things. Believe me, things will surely get worse. But at least you will be beginning what should have been done 2 years ago.

This will certainly make everyone happy, be a great relief for you, and here in the Land you'd have much support, and there'd be great relief at home. We have grown here to 60 children; they have become strong and good workers, and their parents are very happy about that.

If you want to explore another avenue to come here, and if there is anything I can do to make things easier, write me.

Well, the latest news I can give you is that I got married this week. I have found what I've been seeking for so long and am very happy and content. My wife is Mirjam Weizmann, she is a musician and she manages the Kindergarden. She came a few months ago to Ein Charod. We got to know each other and we married, without a *shadchen* [marriage broker] and without the usual ceremonies. Marriage celebrations here are very simple, and therefore more natural, involving the whole community (I will be writing to Eva with details.) I'm enclosing photographs so you can get to know her.

Things are going well for me. I've become healthier and stronger, I feel that being single and waiting till now was fortunate, because today, married, I have no worries, and my wife and I have been granted a different future than the one before.

My wish is that we see each other soon, hopefully the appropriate way will present itself so that you, with wife and children, will be worry-free, and with a better future ahead. Be all heartfelt greeted and kissed,

from your **Yechezkel**

MISSING PIECES

Yechezkel to sister-in-law Ella in Berlin
Kibbutz Ein Charod, Palestine, ca. 1937

Dear Ella, Shalom!

After a long time, once again I'm writing directly to you. My reason for this is the statement in your letter that you intend to send Sigmund and Josef into a Yeshiva here. What kind of thinking is this? What should be the outcome of this – What future do you see in this for your children?

Here I see everything in black and white: in Jerusalem one sees these "holy ones" with pale faces, close to starving, preferring to beg rather than learn a craft, or go to work, always hoping for a miracle!

The only so called "miracle" that does appear benefits only the father of these holy "sprouts" who brokers transactions with rental fees and earns interest from these youngsters, and afterwards they go into the "Yeshiva" and become even more holy, because they go around with *peyes* [side curls] and beards. This is how these "sponges" deceive us working people into supporting them in their "hard-earned" goals.

Do you think, dear Ella, that with people like this one can build a Homeland for our people who are languishing in *golus* [the world outside Palestine]? Do you see any future in this? While I respect and value each *frommen* [religious person],

24

they undermine what we're trying to do; these youths are useless for the building of the land. That is: coming here they will simply be going from one misery to another.

Sigmund and Josef, like all the others, should learn a craft, work, and become good workers, if you don't want this, then it's preferable they remain in *golus*, rather than come here and be even more lost and thus create a hateful future for themselves. We can no longer follow the ways of our parents who would continue to follow those kind of ways here, else we will all perish.

My heart was pounding yesterday when I saw 60 boys and girls arrive here, fresh from Germany, but with none of my "very holy" relatives among them: no Sigmund, no Josef, no Martha and no Sophie, — their dear Mother Ella protecting her little children so that they learn to starve a little longer and maybe wait through one more political crisis. Then what?

My anger is because you, dear Ella, till now have not set out on the right way even though I stated this more than a year ago. Dear Noah! I still have not heard your opinion and I shouldn't accuse so much, but this is what's right.

And so, about me and Mirjam I can give you the best news, we are healthy and happy with life, and we are engaged both spiritually and culturally.

In a few months I will surely be able to give you happy tidings.

Till then, heartfelt greetings and kisses from your

Yechezkel

Yechezkel died in 1948 during Israel's War of Independence.

MISSING PIECES

PART 2
From the *Polenaktion* to the Warsaw Ghetto Uprising
Family Circumstances and Historical Events[12]
October 28, 1938 – May 16, 1943

Two events were particularly relevant to the experiences and fate of Weinreb and Isaak family members before and during World War II. The first was the *Polenaktion*, which resulted in the October 1938 expulsion of approximately 17,000 Jewish residents holding Polish passports. The second was Operation Barbarossa, which began during the summer of 1941. Operation Barbarossa was the code name given to the invasion of the Soviet Union by Nazi Germany.[13] The invasion led to a major escalation of the *Einsatzgruppen* and the beginning of mass murder.[14]

Josef and Sigmund Weinreb were victims of both the *Polenaktion* and the *Einsatzgruppen*.

A description of these events and their impact on family members follows. The correspondence from June 1938 through July 1942 is presented chronologically in Part 3 of this volume.

The *Polenaktion* [5,7]
October 28-29, 1938

Hitler's goal of making Germany *Judenfrei* (free of Jews) became increasingly difficult to achieve with the annexation of Austria and the Sudetenland in Czechoslovakia in 1938. A significant number of Jews living in Germany had taken refuge in Austria during the rise of Hitler and the Nazi Party, and now Austria was part of the German Reich. Thus, many thousands of Jews in both countries were in desperate need of securing safe refuge elsewhere at a time when neighboring countries had imposed strict limits on immigration.

In anticipation of the unwelcome return of Polish Jews living in the German Reich, the Polish government decreed in October 1938 that the passports of Polish nationals who had been living abroad for more than five years without interruption would be invalidated on October 30. In response, Nazi officials ordered the immediate expulsion Jews holding valid Polish passports.

During the early morning hours of October 28, 1938, Noah Weinreb and his sons, Sigmund and Josef, were arrested at their home in Berlin and taken to the Alexanderplatz Police Station. In his memoir, Lazarus (Leslie), who was age 11 at the time, describes watching the scene through a peephole in the door of the room he shared with Josef.[15]

By morning, Noah, Sigmund and Josef had been deported to the border town of Zbaszyn, Poland. According to the description of the expulsion in the *Memorial Book–Victims of the Persecution of Jews under the National Socialist Tyranny in Germany 1933-1945* in the German Federal Archives (*Das Bundesarchiv*), there are limited records pertaining to the immediate fate of those affected.[16] Pinkas Isaak was also arrested, though not expelled. His circumstances are detailed on page 35 of this volume.

The *Polenaktion* was underway across Germany. In Leipzig, Alter Meier Isaak was deported as well on October 28, 1938, according to the *Memorial Book–Victims of the Persecution of Jews under the National Socialist Tyranny in Germany 1933-1945* in the German Federal Archives (*Das Bundesarchiv*). He remains among the thousands whose fate immediately after the expulsion has not been determined, though records in the Central Database of Shoah Victims' Names at Yad Vashem indicate that he was in Lodz, Poland, at some point during the war.[17] The record states that he was murdered.

Operation Barbarossa and the *Einsatzgruppen* [18]
Summer 1941

The Baltic States (Lithuania, Latvia, and Estonia) were invaded and occupied by Soviet forces during the summer of 1940. Thus, they were Soviet republics when Nazi Germany invaded the Soviet Union in June 1941. Once again, the number of Jews under Nazi control increased significantly. It was with the invasion of the Soviet Union that the calculated mass murder of European Jewry by the *Einsatzgruppen* began. Sigmund and Josef were in Vilna and Kuršėnai in Lithuania during this time.

With the invasion of Poland in 1939, the *Einsatzgruppen* (special action groups of the SS Intelligence Service) were responsible for carrying out security measures in newly occupied territories as Nazi Germany moved across Europe. However, the *Einsatzgruppen* are most closely associated with the "mobile killing units" deployed in the Soviet territories. While victims included Roma, Communist and Soviet officials, and Soviet prisoners of war, Jews of every age and gender were the primary targets.[18]

Following the invasion of the Soviet Union in June 1941, the increased scale of *Einsatzgruppen* operations led to the annihilation of entire Jewish communities. With the enthusiastic assistance of local collaborators, police units and the *Schutzstaffel-Waffen* (SS) rounded up countless men, women, and children, who were taken to designated sites, stripped of their belongings, and shot into empty pits. It is estimated that *Einsatzgruppen* were responsible for the murder of more than 1.5 million Holocaust victims in Soviet territories.[18]

When Nazi Germany invaded the Soviet Union on June 22, 1941, and the town of Kuršėnai a short time later, attempts to escape to Russia through Latvia were generally unsuccessful. Accusing the Jews of supporting the Soviets, Lithuanian nationalists subjected them to extreme cruelty and humiliating forced labor. Jewish men aged 12 and older were held for a week in the *beit midrash* (Jewish study hall). On July 16, 1941, 150 Jewish men were taken to the forest nearby, where they were shot into a ditch.[19]

Based on these findings and the timing of their last dated correspondence, it is likely that the undated final letter from Josef and Sigmund was written in Kuršėnai during the late spring or early summer of 1941. The translation of that letter can be found on pages 78 and 79 of this volume.

Sigmund and Josef Weinreb

There is no official record of Sigmund or Josef in the *Memorial Book–Victims of the Persecution of Jews under the National Socialist Tyranny in Germany 1933-1945* in the German Federal Archives (*Das Bundesarchiv*). The only traceable records include testimony given to Yad Vashem in Jerusalem by their aunt and a request for information that was submitted to the International Red Cross by their sister Martha. What we know about their experiences comes from the letters and cards contained in the tattered brown envelope.

Photographs in the authors' private collection

Sigmund and Josef made their way from Zbaszyn to Warsaw, where they met with their older brother Leopold, who had immigrated to Palestine in 1934 and returned to Europe sometime later. As described on page 32 of this volume, Leopold instructed them to leave Warsaw and proceed to Vilna, where he planned to meet them. The letter written by Josef in March 1940 makes it clear that they were still waiting for Leopold, though months had passed.

The correspondence from Sigmund and Josef describes the hardships they endured yet resonates with hope for a better future. Their final letters introduce Sigmund's bride Toibe, who added a note to her new mother-in-law. Both Sigmund and Josef planned to join the Russian Army. This was not to be.

The last communication from the brothers was sent from the village of Kuršėnai, Lithuania, where the events described on page 29 suggest the details and timing of their murder. A monument stands outside Kuršėnai in the Padarbiu forest at the site of the mass grave where the victims are buried. While the details inscribed on the plaque are not precisely aligned with the historical documentation, its presence reminds us that a Jewish community lived in Kuršėnai (Kurshan) 80 years ago.[20]

Photograph of the monument erected in memory of the Jews of Kurshan, located at the site of the mass grave in the Padarbiu forest

Rosin, Joseph: *Protecting our Litvak Heritage*, p.108
Photograph used with permission

A plaque on the monument bears an inscription in Yiddish. Translation:
"At this site Hitler's assassins and their local helpers murdered 100 Kurshan Jewish men on 22 July, 1941."

Rosin, Joseph: *Protecting our Litvak Heritage*, p.108
Photograph used with permission

Leopold (Leo) Weinreb

Leopold immigrated to Palestine in 1934 and returned to Europe at some point thereafter. From a letter written by Josef, dated March 28, 1940, it is clear that Leopold was in Warsaw before the beginning of World War II. Thus, he was not directly affected by the *Polenaktion* but was brought together with Sigmund and Josef in 1939 as a result.

While in Palestine, Leopold joined the Irgun *(Irgun Ze'vai Le'umi)*. Josef's letter of March 28, 1940, suggests the likely nature of Leopold's work with the Irgun in Warsaw. The organization's activities included the procurement of arms for the struggle in Palestine.[21,2] The translation of that letter can be found on page 58 of this volume.

Leo, 1933 [Age 18]

Photograph in the authors' private collection

When Sigmund and Josef arrived in Warsaw, Leopold directed them to leave the city for their own safety and proceed to Vilna, where he would meet them later. This plan did not materialize. Josef indicates that Leo served in the Polish Army, though the timing is unclear.

The first correspondence from Leopold appears on page 54 in this volume. It is a Rosh Hashanah greeting printed in Palestine in 1938. Additional correspondence begins on page 80, with a letter dated October 26, 1941, sent on his behalf from the Warsaw ghetto.

While the final letter from Leopold is dated 1942, official records held in the *Memorial Book—Victims of the Persecution of Jews under the National Socialist Tyranny in Germany 1933-1945* in the German Federal Archives (*Das Bundesarchiv*) state that he was murdered in the Majdanek concentration camp in June 1943. Thus, we know that he survived and likely fought in the Warsaw ghetto uprising.[22] Of the Jewish resistance fighters remaining in the ghetto after May 16, 1943, the last day of the uprising, approximately 18,000 were deported to the Majdanek concentration camp.[23]

Leopold's letters speak of positive events as well as the often insurmountable challenges he encountered daily. Most notably, he writes of his marriage to Bina and the birth of their daughter Rachel. According to information provided by surviving family members, Bina and the baby died in the ghetto.

"Struggles and Martyrdom"
Monument at the entry gate of the Majdanek concentration camp
Photograph in the authors' private collection, 2015

Noah Weinreb

On October 28, 1938, Noah was arrested and deported to Zbaszyn, Poland, where he was detained until January 1939. At that time, he was permitted to return to Berlin for reasons that are not entirely clear. The letters written by Ella and Noah in the aftermath of the *Polenaktion* describe what occurred during the months that followed.

By the winter of 1939, the Weinreb children were no longer in Berlin. Eva had married and was living in Portugal. Leo was likely in Warsaw. Martha and her new husband Pinkas had arrived in London following a stay of several weeks in Italy. Sophie had secured employment in London, which enabled her to obtain a visa. Josef and Sigmund had been deported to Zbaszyn, and their location was unknown. A visa had been secured for Jenny to enter Portugal, where she was living with her sister Eva. The two youngest children, Lazarus and Benno, had been admitted to England on the strength of a letter written by Pinkas Isaak and his brother, Rabbi Bernhard Isaak.[24]

Following Noah's return from Zbaszyn, he and Ella sought refuge in Hungary. Ella, whose parents were born in Hungary, had been able to obtain the necessary documentation for herself but not for Noah. They began the journey nonetheless but were not successful. Noah was removed from the train and sent back to Berlin. He instructed Ella to proceed to Hungary, in the hope that she would be able to secure the required documentation and send for him at a later date. Noah was arrested again on September 21, 1939. He was sent to the Sachsenhausen concentration camp, where he was murdered on May 3, 1940.

The last communication from Noah is written on a fragment of paper that was likely smuggled out of the camp. The translation of that message can be found on page 66 of this volume.

Noah Weinreb
Nuremberg, 1922

Photograph in the authors' private collection

Pinkas Isaak

Pinkas was arrested on October 28, 1938, only seven weeks after his marriage to Martha. He was unable to present his passport, as he and Martha had given their Polish passports along with a financial consideration to an individual who had promised to secure transit visas for them. These visas were intended to ensure their entry into Italy as an interim stop on the way to a final destination elsewhere. Because the deportation order applied to residents with a Polish passport and Pinkas did not have his passport available, he was taken from the police station to prison and then released. He narrowly escaped a second arrest.

Photograph in the Collection of
The Museum of Jewish Heritage – A Living Memorial to the Holocaust, New York, NY
Gift of Beth Gerson and M. David Isaak

When their properly endorsed passports arrived, Martha and Pinkas prepared to leave Germany without delay. They departed on December 4, 1938. Shortly thereafter, the police descended on the family home again, only to find that Pinkas and Martha had vanished. The details of these events are documented in their memoir, *Our Story: Martha & Pinkas Isaak*.[25]

Resilience and Rebuilding

After the war, surviving Isaak and Weinreb family members settled in England, Israel, and America. They were no longer neighbors, making family celebrations especially meaningful.

Perhaps no gathering has been more important than the celebration honoring the return of Leo Margulies, who survived the Buchenwald concentration camp. The camp was liberated by United States forces in April 1945. Before reuniting with his family in London, Leo traveled with a group of orphaned children to France, where he remained with them until they had been placed in proper care.

The family gathering was a celebration of resilience, purpose, dignity and hope.

Celebrating the Return of Leo Margulies
London, 1946

Photograph in the authors' private collection

The author, M. David Isaak, is the small boy on the lower left. His parents, Martha and Pinkas Isaak, are standing behind him. The honoree is the fourth person from the right in the second row.

MISSING PIECES

PART 3

Guide to the Correspondence: 1935 – 1942

1935	Yechezkel, Palestine, to Eva, Berlin	20
1937	Yechezkel, Palestine, to Noah, Berlin	22
1937	Yechezkel, Palestine, to Ella, Berlin	24
1938, Jun 1	Hinda, Palestine, to Eva, Lisbon	40
1939, Aug 7	Josef, Vilna, to Family, Lisbon	42
1939, Aug 12	Noah, Berlin, to Children, Lisbon	44
1939, Sep 12	Noah, Berlin, to Ella, Hungary	45
1939, Sep 13	Noah, Berlin, to Ella, Hungary	46
1939, Sep 19	Noah, Berlin, to Ella, Hungary	47
1939, Oct 9	Ella, Hungary, to Eva & Julius, Lisbon	50
1938	Leopold, Palestine, to Eva & Julius, Lisbon	54
1940, Jan 23	Hinda, Palestine, to Eva, Lisbon	55
1940, Mar 12	Hinda, Palestine, to Eva, Lisbon	56
1940, Mar 6	Sigmund, Vilna, to Ella, Lisbon	57
1940, Mar 28	Josef, Vilna, to Eva, Lisbon	58
1940, Apr 22	Sigmund, Šiauliai, to Ella, Lisbon	64
1940	Noah, Sachsenhausen, to Rachel, Berlin	66
1940, Jul 14	Jeny, Berlin, to Eva, Lisbon	68
1940, Sep 10	Josef, Kuršėnai, to Rachel, Berlin	70
1940, Nov 15	Sigmund, Kuršėnai, to Rachel, Berlin	70
1940, Nov 14	Sigmund, Kuršėnai, to Ella, Lisbon	71
1940	Mali, London, to Ella, Lisbon	72
1941, May 8	Josef, Kuršėnai, to Eva & Julius, Lisbon	74
1941, May 15	Sigmund, Kuršėnai, to Ella, Lisbon	76
1941	Sigmund, Kuršėnai, to Ella, Lisbon	78
1941, Oct 26	Izydor, Warsaw, to Ella & Family, Lisbon	80
1942, Feb 2	Leo, Warsaw, to Ella & Family, Lisbon	81
1942, Apr 21	Leo, Warsaw, to Eva, Lisbon	82
1942, Jul 6	Leo, Warsaw, to Eva, Lisbon	83

MISSING PIECES

Hinda (Noah's Mother) to granddaughter Eva in Portugal
June 1, 1938, Old Age House, Afulah, Palestine

> Shalom,
>
> My dear heart-loved little children Chava [Eva] and Julius untill 120. You should always be healthy, in *mazeldik* [lucky] times, with happy hearts and happiness filled futures, Amen.

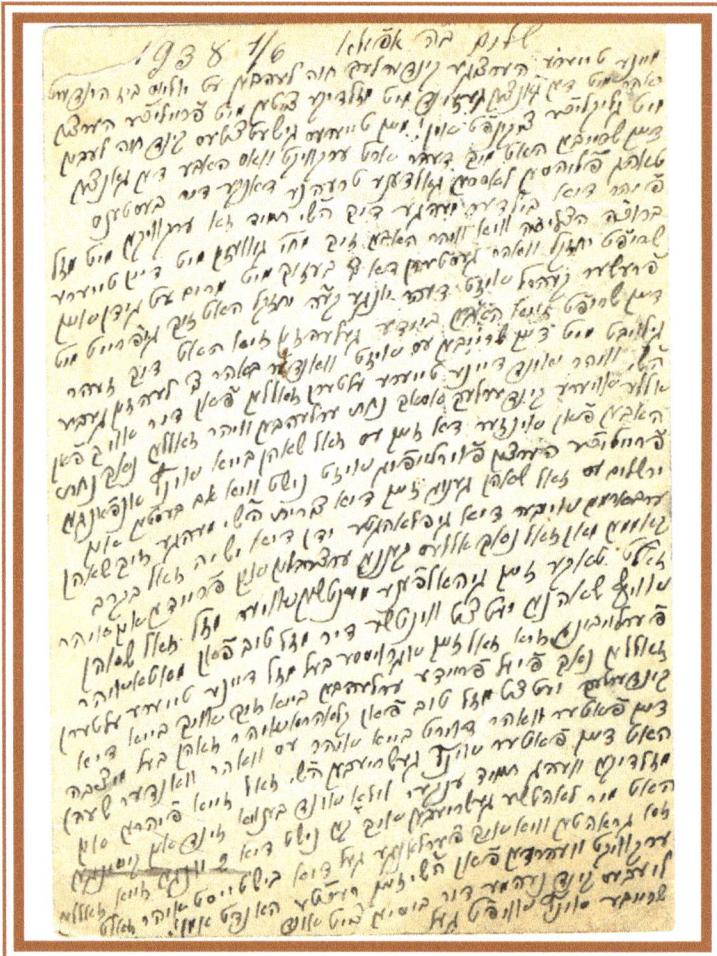

> My dearest, treasured child Chava, your letter, which I read all day, brought golden tears to my eyes. Thank you especially for the pictures — may God always afford you *mazel* [good luck], blessings and success for the pleasure you brought us with your letter.
>
> Yechezkel visited here yesterday with Miriam and Gideon — a refreshing kid is that young one, with God's blessing. Yechezkel enjoyed your letter that they both read. He very much believed what you wrote. It is wonderful when you write, we and your dear parents should always

have much *naches* [pride] from you and your little children, as we too should have here from ours.

Right now things are not at their best and we should begin soon to have a more joyous future, it is already enough with the *tzuros* [woes], the good Lord should have mercy on the persecuted Jews, the salvation should come already — we should be able to relate everything in freedom.

Mazel Tov from Klara, your Father was there by her, it was wonderful, your Father wrote. God should lead them all on the right path, including Lulu [Leslie] and Benno.

Dear child, take a little time and write to us often, right? — You'll

surely have a big *mitzvah* [good deed]; we're always standing and looking out for the mail so we'll at least have a little to talk about.

Be healthy and live in fortunate times and you should also also be strong, and you should have a heap of money, and you should not have to be stingy to anyone who knocks on your door; and you should still have a heap of money left over. You understand? We do too. Be healthy, with fortunate business, dear Julius (Eva's husband) should always be successful.

Grandmother **Hinda Weinreb**, Old Age House, Afula, Palestine.

Dear Children, I write an extra line and greet you and bless you — you should always be fortunate and successful and make a good living.

Your grandfather, **Avrohom Weinreb**.

MISSING PIECES

Postcard from Josef (age 17) to family in Lisbon
General Post Office, Vilna, Poland, August 7, 1939

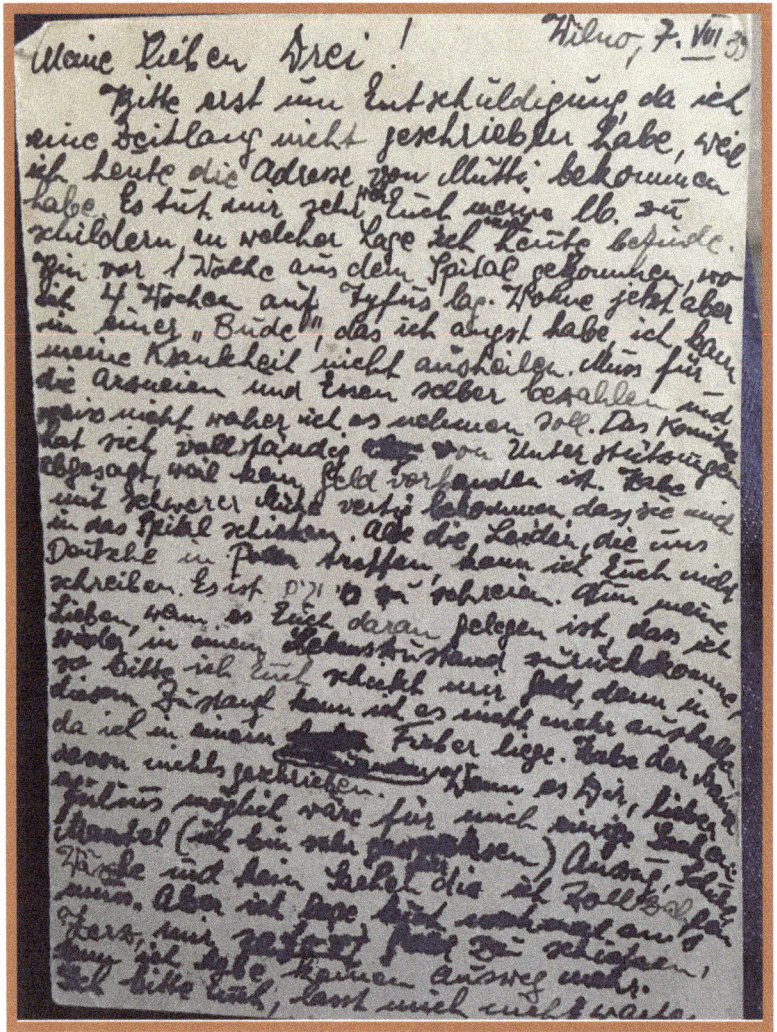

A FAMILY STORY RETOLD

My dear Three! (Sisters Eva and Jenny, Brother–in–Law Julius)

First of all, please forgive me for not having written for a long time, because I just got Mutti's (Ella) address today.

It pains me very much my dears to describe the state I find myself in today. I'm one week out of the hospital in which I had spent 4 weeks with typhus. I have to pay by myself for the medicines and food and don't know where I can get the money.

The committee (Joint Distribution Commitee) has completely stopped its support because no money is available. It was with great effort that I had them agree to send me to the hospital. All the suffering that we Germans encounter in Poland I can't even describe to you. It makes you want to scream "*chai v'kayam*" ["lives forever"]. So my loved ones, if it suits you, in order for me to 'come back to life', I beg of you to send me money because I can no longer hold out like this; I still have a high fever. I've not written anything about this to Mama.

If possible for you, dear Julius, send me a few things: A coat (I have grown a lot), a suit, underwear – but no things on which I would have to pay customs fees. I hope if I touched your heart you will send me money immediately because I have no other resource.

I beg of you, don't make me wait, as I go every day to the Post Office hoping to receive your response. I would like to be healthier, then Mama could come to Vilna in 2 or 3 weeks to visit me.

Dear Eva and dear Julius, pray that the 'Highest One' responds to me. Stay healthy. I hope that will soon apply to me as well.

Greetings to dear Jenny, and for you, greetings and kisses,

Josef

Several factors strongly suggest that this postcard was not written autonomously:

- The postcard was sent from Poland prior to World War II but bears a German postage stamp.
- The handwriting of the address is distinctly different from that of the message.
- Sigmund is not mentioned in the message, though other correspondence suggests that he and Josef traveled together as they made their way from Zbaszyn to Warsaw. (See: Letter dated March 6, 1940, where Vilna is not mentioned)
- It is unlikely that Josef was seriously ill in Vilna in August and extinguishing fires in Warsaw one month later during the German bombing of that city. (See: Letter dated March 6, 1940)
- The Hebrew expression that translates "lives forever" is inappropriate in this context.
- Given the circumstances, a visit by Josef's mother is illogical. By now, Ella had taken refuge in Hungary. Josef's father, Noah Weinreb, had been sent back to Berlin and would be arrested.

Noah and Ella to Children in Portugal
Berlin, August 12, 1939

My dear children till 120 yrs.!

We received your letter with great joy, and greatly enjoyed the "enclosure."

It's unfortunate that we have to be apart, at least let us always hear good news from each other.

Now it's almost 4 weeks of my being here [Noah and Ella were staying in her parents' house]..

After a few months we will finally be able to leave Berlin. The passport for Mutti [mother] was applied for about 3 months ago. She also has the "stamp." This week she will call the Visa office. Perhaps I'll be successful in getting one as well, naturally it will only be good for 30 days. I will notify you about this. Mali (Ella's sister) will be traveling this week to London.

Dear Eva, I'll take care of your wish as soon as all the running about has subsided.

Dear …. is also trying to get to London. Leo and Mali Margulies have already received their Permits. We have, thank God, good news from Martha, Sofie and the boys. We hope all of you continue to have the best well-being, be blessed and kissed, have success in everything,

Your Father.

Special kisses to my first little grandchildren [long life to them]! Have you, dear Jenny, sent the …. to Aunt Toni? Why don't you give us an answer about this? Don't you know her address anymore? *T. Binder Tel Aviv, 2 Joel Street*
So, don't forget!

Dear Children,

I hope to give you some good news soon. Dear children, be so kind and send Josef 20 zlote. It is very urgent: *Josef Weinreb, Poland, Wilna, General Post Office.* Leo and Josef are together.

And Jenny, please send the 20 zlote soon. Greetings and kisses to my beloved children,

Mutti [Mom]

Noah in Berlin to Ella in Hungary
Berlin, September 12, 1939

My beloved, dear Ella till 120 yrs.

I arrived here at noon today and all is, thank God, in perfect order. Your card to me arrived at the same time which gave me great joy; it made me think we have not been torn apart.

It is also our fate that we are not meant to be together for Rosh Hashanah.

Thank God I'm still free and I pray to God to protect me from any *tzores* [bad things]. Don't worry if you do not hear from me right away, one cannot know what tomorrow brings. Tomorrow I'm going to see about the cargo problem from last week and hope to God they won't give me any hinderance. Isak (Fluss' son) is here, dear Mutti (Rachel Rottenberg]) will probably go to Jeny (Fluss) for the *Yom-Tov* [holy day].

From there, could you get an Entry permit for me for 6 months? If I have an Entry permit the Police would give me an Exit permit to get to Hungary. Without it, one cannot get out of here. Such is the present law.

Be healthy, pray and ask God for a healthy, good, *mazeldiges* [lucky] year. We should not know any more bad things. All *tzores* [woes] should remain far away from us and all *Jehudim* [Jews].

Blessings and kisses, **Noah.**

Additional writing, upside down at top of card:

"**The entry permit – you understand?**" Please convey to all my family: (In Hebrew and Yiddish): May you be written in for a good year with good livelihood and all good things.

Noach

A FAMILY STORY RETOLD

MISSING PIECES

Noah to Ella in Hungary

Berlin, September 13, 1939

My dear special Ella till 120 [Hebrew abbreviation: **Rosh Hashanah Eve**]

I hope you arrived in Miskolc [Hungary] in good health. What last Friday I'd hoped would be granted is here today. Thank God things are still going well for me.

But I must be vigilant every moment. *Hashem* [God] should allow us all to live, and pray for a good year. I got a nice seat in the Sigmundhof Synangogue, *halevai* [hopefully] I'll also be able to lead the service.

Today they released Jeny's (Fluss) boy (Isi) again. **May it be that God will finally show us some mercy.** Grandmother (Rottenberg) looks very bad, she'll be staying with Jeny over Yom-Tov [Holiday].

Where I will be during Yom-Tov and thereafter is in God's hands. May it please God to continue protecting me. Otherwise, nothing's new.

Be blessed and kissed my dear Ella. **Pray to God we'll see each other in good health again and together enjoy our children who are now scattered in the world,** and be able, in peace, to relate all our *tzores* [travails]. Tell the children where I am so at least they'll be a little reassured.

Where are the boys?

To the dear relatives, many heartfelt greetings and a deservedly healthy year. I hope they'll not be resentful of your visit – what can one do… I thank in advance those who are taking care of you. I'm really happy that you, dear Ella, are there.

Your **Noach**

Again, best greetings and many kisses with all good things,.

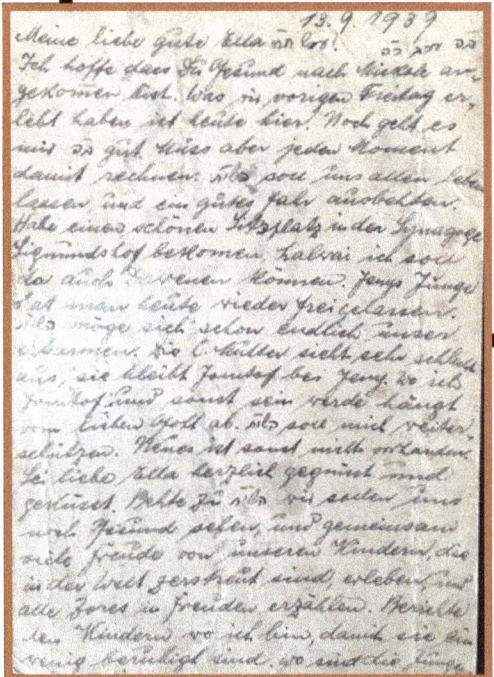

A FAMILY STORY RETOLD

Noah to Ella in Hungary

Berlin, September 19, 1939

Very honored family: I wish you *G'mar Chatimah Tovah* ["Good Inscription"] and that all *Yehudim* [Jews] should be helped. Can't write much today — see that my wife is not upset. God will help soon. *Good Yom-Tov*, **Weinreb**

Dearest, precious, Ella, till 120 yrs. [In Hebrew: Good "inscription"— for Yom Kippur]

I'm worried not having received any message from you in response to my two cards. Hopefully you are alright. Eva has written to Grossman — we need to write her where we are located. You should write her from there immediately and tell her where we are.

Dearest, most kind, Ella, if you don't receive any correspondence from me in the next days, you must not be upset. I have to register today with the Police and I will be sent to where they send all the Poles. May Blessed God safeguard us all. You can write dear *Mutti* (Rachel Rottenberg), she will quickly be able to give you more details. Hopefully I'll be able to write and give you good news.

Best greetings and kisses, please pray for a good year and pray also for me and our children. **I'm happy that I was able to spend Rosh Hashanah in freedom. Where I'm going to be from now on only God knows**.

So again, heartfelt kisses and all good things. Hopefully in Budapest you accomplished good things.

Your Noah

See page 48 for the photograph of the back of this postcard.

19.9.39 ב"ה

Liebe teuere Ella לאי. Ich bin besorgt von dir auf meine 2 Karten gar keine Nachricht bekomen zu haben. Hoffentlich bist du gesund. Boa יצ' hat zu Grossmann geschrieben man solle ihr schreiben wo wir uns befinden. Du sollst ihr von dort sofort schreiben wo wir sind. liebe gute Ella יצ' wenn du von mir in den nächsten Tagen kein Schreiben bekomen solltest, sollst du nicht aufgeregt sein. Ich muss mich heute bei der Polizei melden, und werde da hinkomen wo alle polnische hingekomen sind. השי"ת wird uns alle schützen. Du kannst zu der l. Mutter schreiben, sie wird dir sofort eine Antwort geben. Hoffentlich werde ich dir gute Nachricht mitteilen können. Sei gesund, gegrüsst und geküsst, halte dir aus ein gutes Pets. und bete auch für mich und unseren Kindern. Ich freue mich dass ich die Rosch-Haschana Tage frei durchgebracht habe. Wo ich Jankiper sein werde weiss Gott. Also nochmals herzliche Küsse und alles Gute. Hoffentlich hast du in Budapest alles gute erledigt Dein Nandi

Noah did not have the required documentation when he attempted unsuccessfully to take refuge in Hungary. In her memoir, Ella and Noah's daughter Jenny indicates that her father was offered a falsified document, which he declined because he feared reprisal if he was caught.[26] Noah was taken off the train and returned to Berlin.

The correspondence between Ella and Noah expresses their anguish and concern. Ella laments decisions made under circumstances that were well beyond their control. The last postcard from Noah, which was written as he was about to report to the police station, explains that he had been instructed "to report today." His final words were written on a scrap of paper that was likely smuggled out of the camp.

Letters and postcards from various family members, including Sigmund and Josef, reference Noah's death. The reader is reminded that, apart from Eva, who was living in neutral Portugal, each writer was aware of only his or her own circumstances throughout these tumultuous years.

MISSING PIECES

Ella to daughter Eva & Julius in Lisbon
Miskolc, Hungary, October 9, 1939

My Beloved Children, till 120

I read your letter with great joy. I spent a long time happily reading it. It has been about 7 weeks now that I daily have been awaiting the Letter Carrier. My beloved children, I hope you have all prayed to have a *G'mar Tov* [Yom Kippur blessing: "Good Outcome"]. You should hear from me and everyone, only the best. Please God, begin the New Year only with "Good."

I was in Budapest over Rosh Hashanah in a very beautiful and *frum* [religious] synagogue like the one in Sigmundhof, only 4 times as big, with a fabulous *chazen* [cantor] and a choir, just as I like it. The choir consisted of little boys, singing like canaries. I heard God in a good place, I was happy to stand from 6 in the morning until 2, and I drank a sip of milk. I prayed with the greatest devotion but the good things I wished for have not happened yet.

I'm so alone without my husband and children, it is such a tragedy. I know nothing about dear Papa and my dear children in Warsaw, and in Wilna, where dear Sigmund and Leo and Josef are. Unfortunately, to this day, I know nothing about them.

At least this time our Dear blessed God should have mercy; I have suffered so much, and I cannot stop myself from crying. I don't know from where my strength comes. Surely Blessed God will help soon, and Blessed God has heard my earnest prayers for all my children, and Uncle and Sister-in-Law should have a good outcome, and of course also for your dear Papa.

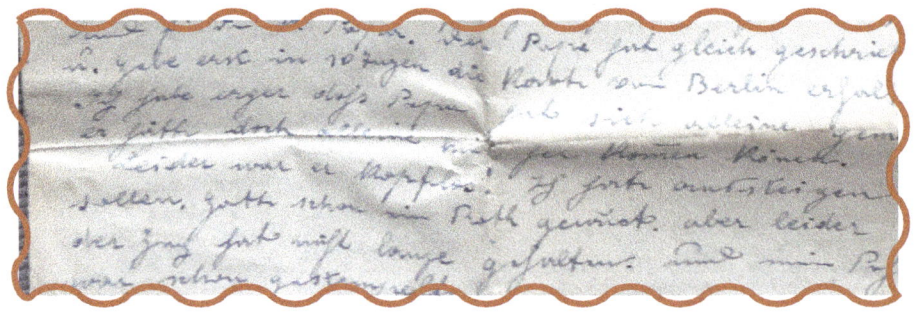

SEGMENT OF THE FOUR-PAGE LETTER

A FAMILY STORY RETOLD

> **Papa wrote right away that he had taken a train to Berlin. I'm troubled that he went back, he could probably have come here later by himself. Unfortunately, he lost his head! I should have stepped off the train, I realize now. But unfortunately the train's stop was not long, and my Pass had already been stamped.**
>
> …(Description of items) placed in a large box: Papa's fur-coat with men's suits, dresses in a hat box, and other items in a handbag….**Papa had with him only his shirts and his good gabardine overcoat, and unfortunately nothing else. God should help that he will come here soon.**

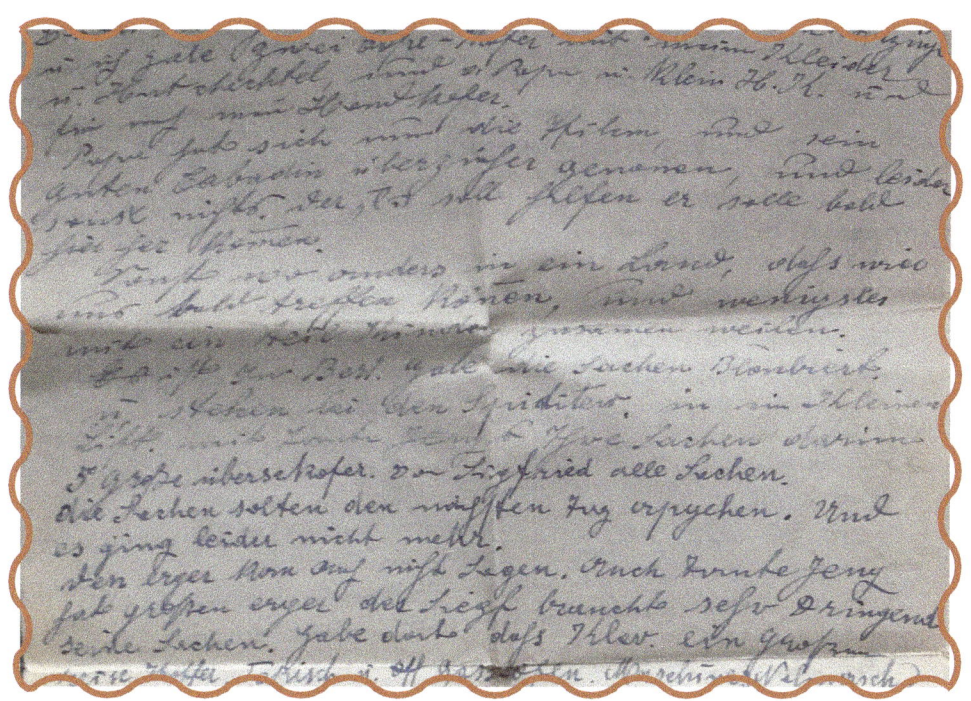

SEGMENT OF THE FOUR-PAGE LETTER

> …Things are different in a land that all we hope for is only to be able to meet, and at least be able to spend some time together. I gave some items to a shipper to place in a small lift (crate), to be put on the train, but unfortunately, that didn't happen.
>
> …The trouble is they lie about it. Siegfried's things were put in 5 large suitcases and were supposed to be shipped the next day, but that didn't happen either. Aunt Jeny (Fluss) is very upset because Siegfried urgently needs his things. I also gave them, to be put in the lift, the piano, a large

trunk, a carpet, gas-oven and sewing machine, cutlery and books and a large box with dresses, underwear and feather-bed covered in a bed-sack.

...The furniture remains in the cellar at dear Oma's [Rottenberg] house, no one wanted to buy them. Dear Martha (Ella's daughter) wrote me that I should send very little, because there's no room there (London). Two good bed sets are also in the cellar at Oma's — it would have cost too much to store in a warehouse.

...I don't know if anything went to London, one has to ask again in a month. I should have sent at least some of the things to Lisbon with Jenny, she could have taken them with her. Well, let this all be for the good. These things are, at the moment, of least importance.

...The main thing is that our Blessed God should present me with a *ness* [miracle] that I should very soon hear from Sigmund, Leo and Josef as well as from dear Papa. We should all be helped.

...Did anyone write about Julius' parents? Have you any letters from dear Sally and Max? Where is Isi (Izydor, Julius' brother)?

...Does anyone perhaps know about our children? ...From Lulu (Leslie) and Benno (the 2 youngest sons) I got a postcard, they are with our children, 5 hours from London in a small village:

L. Weinreb c/o Greenhust, 25 Second Avenue, Chelmsford, Essex, England

...dear Lulu writes joyfully he wishes all a hearty Mazel Tov. Dear Martha wrote me that on September 11th, she gave birth, Bless God, to a boy, and it went, thank God, very easily. This was a very happy letter for me, I have been praying that Martha should make me happy already. The *Seudah* [festive meal – bris] was on September 18th and I got the letter on September 22nd — that letter took about 7 days.

...The boy's name is Moses [Moshe] David after our beloved, blessed Father [Moses Rottenberg] and Pinkas' grandfather. I hope from now on to get only good news from all the children.

...Beloved Eva, I'm very happy that your dear children are so good. I will only be happy when I can finally travel to you.

...Here things are, thank God, very good for me, for eating and sleeping. Here there are 3 cousins of Oma's (Rachel Rottenberg) sister. She is, without bias, 78 years old. Her sons live here, and already they have married children. I'm living at Josef Landau's. They have a son who is serving, and a wonderful daughter Olga who is 18 years old.

...I share with her a beautiful bedroom, very well appointed — they all really like me here and take good care of me. They don't let me be sad, and they have a 12 year old daughter. They are very *frum* [religious] and Modern. All the women here are in *sheitels* [wigs], I am sorry I don't have one, I wear a *tukh* [head scarf]. If I had the money I would buy one immediately.

...I was invited to a *simche* [celebration] by the other cousin – he has little children, the youngest is 6 years old, their place is also very well furnished. He has an old iron business. He's very *Judisch* [Jewish], a splendid example. The Hungarian men are very *frum* as I do so appreciate. Really, a *Yiddishe Malkhus* [Jewish Kingdom], I wish someday I will have the same from my children. Everything good.

...I slept there – the cousin would not let me go home, his wife also is very kind. Nice people, men women and children – that is David Landau. And the third one has no children, married only two years, totally Modern – Wolf Landau. A daughter also lives here, a cousin, who is unfortunately very poor.

...All here are very saddened by what has befallen us. Dear Oma [Rachel Rottenberg] writes to me often, I'm very upset that she has been left alone. For *Yontef* [High Holidays] she is with Fluss. Unfortunately, Isak is also out of town in Hanover. If only Papa would at least be able to write. Blessed God should only rescue us all, I went yesterday to synagogue for the *Rosh Chodesh* [first day of the Jewish month] blessing. God should straighten out what happened to Papa, he should be able come out, with all *Yehudim* [Jews], and I hope we'll all be in a good place with you.

...Despite all, I am very, very anxious here, it is a small place, with about 3000 Jews, about 5 hours journey to Budapest. I hope I get the Post tomorrow. I sent it to Budapest for forwarding.

So, dear beloved, and Julius and dear Ruth and Naomi, many kisses.

Your Mutti

And kisses to my Jenny from your beloved Mother.

Write often!

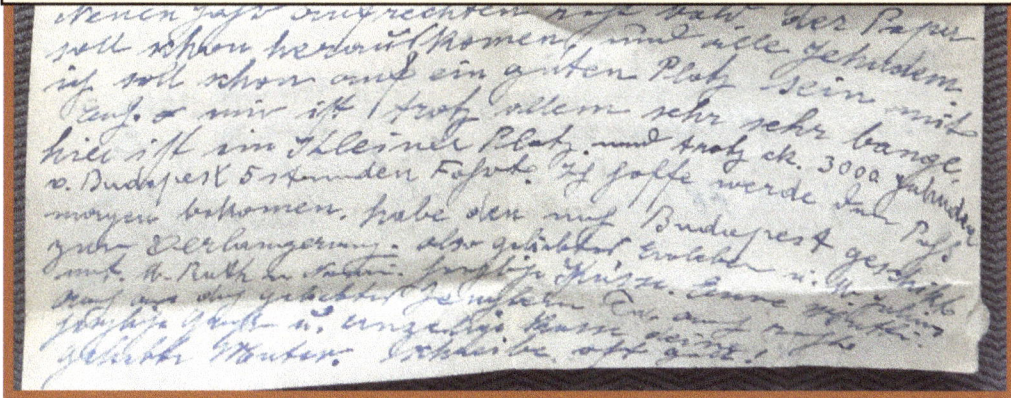

MISSING PIECES

Leopold: Rosh Hashanah Card to sister Eva & Julius Palestine, ca. August, 1938

FRONT   BACK

L'Shana Tovah Tikatevu
[May you be inscribed for a good year].
Taf, Resh, Tzadik, Tet
[Hebrew letters representing the Jewish lunar year 5699]
Mevarech [Blesses]
Eliezer [Leo] ***Weinreb***

Dear Sister and dear Brother-In-Law,
　　Please accept my many apologies that I have not let you hear from me for so long, but I will catch up. My belated thanks to you for the attention you've shown me. Heartfelt greetings and kisses,
　　　　　　　　　　　Your **Leo**

This Rosh Hashanah greeting is the first communication from Leopold Weinreb in this volume. It was printed in Palestine in 1938. (The lunar Hebrew calendar year 5699 straddles the Gregorian calendar years 1938-1939.)

Leopold joined the underground Irgun [*Irgun Ze'vai Le'umi*] in Palestine and was imprisoned for a time for his involvement in the organization's activities, which included procuring arms and facilitating the immigration of Jews from Eastern Europe to Palestine beyond the strict limits imposed by the British authorities.[27, 2]

The letter written by Josef in March 1940 describes the brothers' meeting with Leopold in Warsaw during the invasion of Poland. The remaining correspondence from Leopold was sent from the Warsaw ghetto in 1941 and 1942. Surviving family members have confirmed that Leopold's wife Bina and their baby daughter Rachel died in the ghetto. Records in the German Federal Archives and Yad Vashem indicate that Leopold was deported to the Majdanek concentration camp, where he was murdered in June 1943.

Hinda (Noah's Mother) to granddaughter Eva in Portugal
Elder House #3, Afulah, Palestine, Jan 23, 1940

My beloved dear child Chava (Eva),

I'm very worried because you have given me no answer to my letter: What have you heard about your dear Father? Have you received any information? Yechezkel (Noah's brother) can't make any sense of it.

Our blessed God should have mercy on you with *mazeldicke* [lucky] assistance, my dear child.

Believe me, we already have enough *tzouros* [troubles] going around, but we must really hope and have trust that our Father in Heaven will not, *chas v'chalilah* ["perish the thought"], abandon his children.

But, my dear child, patience and hope have been rewarded for many. Aunt Sarah Schechter from Frankfurt is already in Antwerp, Belgium at Izzy's, and children of the Lerner family still remain in Nuremberg. Yakov and Chava are in *Eretz* [Palestine] at their son's.

Pay good attention, and write to me soon, tell me you and your husband are healthy.

And to dear Ella till 120 years (I wish you) a happy heart together with your husband you should still enjoy a great amount of *naches* [pride] from your dear children together with your husband and we should still be able someday to talk about all this in freedom and with happy hearts, Amen.

Sophie is in Antwerp with her children, Our blessed God should provide her with subsistence – It's not going well for Berta; she washes laundry for people, and he doesn't earn anything, there is no work, may the times get better soon. I wish you well, best of health,

Oma (Grandma) **Hinda Weinreb**

Hinda to granddaughter Eva in Portugal
Palestine, March 12, 1940

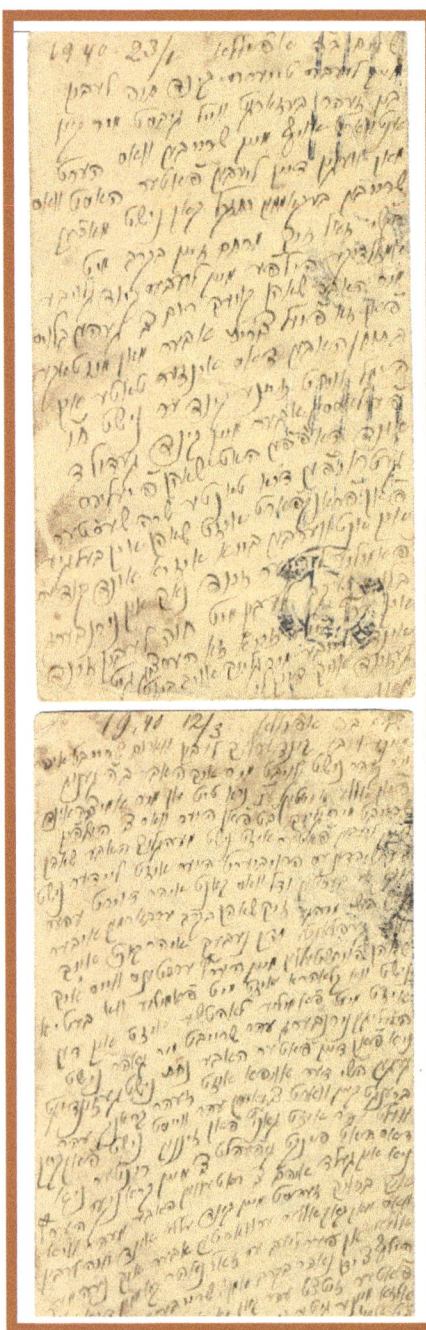

Why is nothing written to me? Believe me, I have, thank God, enough from all sides. Please, do a *mitzvah* [good deed] and write to me immediately — It is not possible from here to do something to help your Father. I have tried various things already, unfortunately, from here it is not the best way, maybe from there you can do something.

May blessed God move soon and have mercy on all Jewish victims, poor things. You can also imagine my heartache. I don't know where Klara and family are, where Betty and family are. Latche is in "holy" Nuremberg — he writes nothing new about your father. I have not sinned against our blessed God.

Opa is very ill he can't put any words together; he knows nothing what goes on in the world, he is without perception — this is really what my poor heart is missing now.

Is money needed to save Noah? I have more than I need. Tell me, my child, Ella, and also Eva, what can we all expect? Perhaps let us hope help will come soon to all. Amen!

Write to me where your father is being held. Perhaps he could write at some time something, right? So my dear Eva write me good news! Amen! How are your little children dear Evaleh? Are you, please God, healthy? Opa wishes extra greetings to all.

Write your mother-in-law something good. What do you hear from your sister (Mali) who lives in England? Even just a few lines. Please greet her and her husband from me.

Oma Hinda Weinreb

Sigmund to mother & siblings
Vilna, Lithuania, March 6, 1940

Dear Mutti and Siblings

You cannot imagine our joy having received your dollars today. 1 dollar here is 5 *Litai* I imagine that by you 1dollar is a lot of money. We thank you very much for this. Healthwise, everything with us is, thank God, good.

Because we are refugees (Jews) we won't be allowed to remain in Wilno; we're going to be sent to the provinces. When? We don't know yet... How are things going with you?

Dear Leo has remained in Warsaw, and today we sent him a card.

By giving English and French lessons here I am earning the minimum necessary for Josef and me to live. Officially, as a refugee, I am not allowed to work. And the possibilities of emigration from here are terrible.

My dear Jennylein, how is it going with you? Are you not yet a *Chasene maydel* [marriage girl]? I have great longing for all of you. Send pictures of yourselves. Be greeted many times and at least kissed by

　　　　　　　　　　　　　　　　Your **Sigmund**

(On the side):"Greetings and kisses, **Josef**"

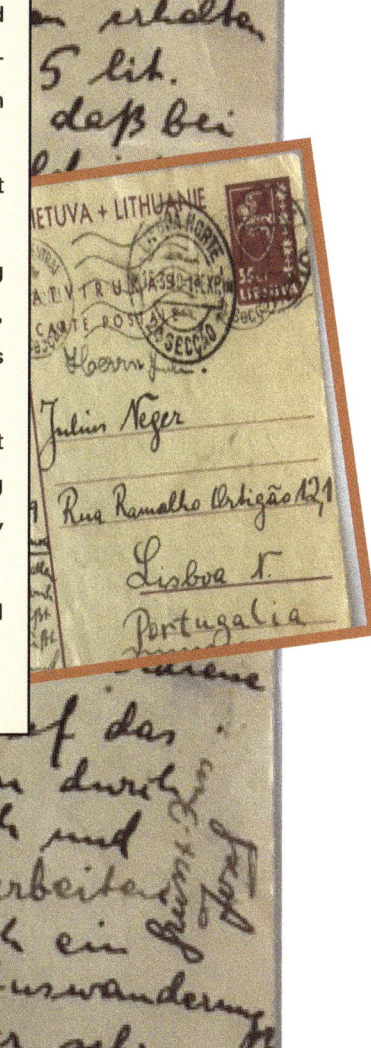

Josef to sister Eva & mother Ella in Lisbon
Vilna, Lithuania, March 28, 1940

I

My dearest ones: *Amv"sh* [till 120 years]

We have received your letter with joy and are very happy, my loved ones, that it goes very well for you, and that our dear Papa *yichyeh* (long may he live) has the possibility to emigrate and join you in Lisbon. (Ed. Note: While there had been plans for Noah to attempt to emigrate and join family in Lisbon, Joseph is unaware his father was interred in the Sachsenhausen concentration camp.) You cannot imagine what joy it is for us for when finally we receive a letter from you, dear Mutti. It lightens our hearts when after a time we get a few lines from our loved ones.

You, dear Eva, write us that we should inform you what we have experienced during the course of the war, and how we fled from Warsaw. Believe me, it's actually not right of me to send to you the terrible experiences that we three brothers have endured.

You should know how, after the Germans came to Warsaw, we fled from there. After Leo returned to Warsaw from the Front (he had volunteered as a Polish officer) and had experienced and gone through some very cruel times, he ordered us to immediately leave Warsaw since we had nothing to eat, not even black bread. Then even during the bombing of Warsaw we had to stand in line, during the night, from 2 am till 10 in the morning during the horrific bombing noises and explosions, with about 2000 other people, in line for a little piece of black bread, which eventually was to be sold to us. Sometimes, after we had lined up since 2 am during the night, in the morning nothing was distributed, and we lost the will to line up again. We would have starved were it not for dear Leo who brought us the little piece of bread he had obtained from his army barracks.

We couldn't even think about sleep; the whole of Warsaw was in flames and we were terrified and had to watch out, standing on the roof with sand pails, standing

Wilno 28. III. 40

I.

Meine Teuren!

Euren lb. Brief haben wir mit Freuden erhalten und sind sehr glücklich darüber, dass es Euch meine lieben sehr gut geht, und das der lb. Papa du Möglichkeit hat zu Euch nach Lisabon zu emigrieren. Ihr könnt Euch nicht vorstellen, was für eine Freude es ist für uns, wenn wir endlich einmal einen Brief von Dir lb. Mutti zu erhalten. Es wird uns leichter auf dem Herz wenn wir nach einer Zeit wieder von unsere Lieben einige Zeilen bekommen. Die lb. Eva schreibst uns wir sollen Euch berichten, was wir im Laufe des Krieges überlebten, und wie wir von Warschau geflüchtet sind. Glaubt mir, es ist eigentlich nicht richtig von mir über solche schreckliche Erlebnisse die wir alle 3 Brüder unterlebt haben Euch zu schildern. Wisse sollt Ihr wie wir, nach dem die Deutschen nach Warschau gekommen sind, von dort geflüchtet sind. — Nachdem Leo von der Front zurückgekommen ist (er hat sich Freiwillig gemeldet als Offizier Polnischer) und sehr grausames durchgemacht hat, befahl er uns sofort Warschau zu verlassen, denn wir hatten nicht einmal Schwarzes Brot zu essen. Denn in der Zeit von der Bombardierung mussten wir in der Nacht von 2 Uhr bis um 10 Uhr früh stehen unter dem schrecklichen Geräusch von Bomben und Harmaten, wo ca. 2000 Menschen standen nach dem Stückchen schwarzen Brot, welches eventuell erst Früh verkauft wurden. Weil schon öfters es möglich war, als wir standen von 2 Uhr nachts, und in der Früh nicht ausgeteilt wurde, haben wir vollkommen den Mut verloren noch einmal zu stehen. Wir wären schon verhungert, wenn nicht der lb. Leo uns gebracht hätte das Stückchen Brot welches er von der Kaserne uns gebracht hätte. An Schlafen war überhaupt nicht zu denken, denn ganz Warschau stand in Flammen, hatten Angst und mussten auch verhüten stehend

II

on a house that was burning terribly, trying to pour the sand on the fire. The fire threatened our house where we stood on the roof, the same as the neighboring house where unfortunately 55 people were burned and buried. That was the assigned duty of every young man, decreed by the Polish government.

Since it had been more than 3 weeks where we were unable to even shut our eyes, we welcomed our friends who relieved us from the dangerous, risky work so we could sleep—and slept for 3 hours. We could not, any longer, bear to watch how the poor young people acting as brave and careful watchmen, were then burned and buried by the bombs—and thus gave their lives for the barbaric Polish people who had already "sold them out."

Leo, (still in the Polish army), begged us to leave Warsaw immediately to avoid the danger of being shot as spies after the Germans came. We took our 2 suitcases packed with laundry, coats, and the suits we had acquired with great difficulty before the war, and, half sad and half happy, we walked through the devastated streets until we ended about 35 km. behind Warsaw, and came to the German-Russian border. We talked to the immigration officer in German, so he let us, and all the things we had brought with us, pass through the neutral zone between Germany and Russia. Our joy was so great that we almost cried, since we knew some others had been locked up or had everything confiscated when they tried to cross the border.

It was 5 in the afternoon as the two of us lay there, and we saw, through the forest path, the Russian border. But suddenly, as it was already dark, some "Pollak" (sic) farmers jumped up from the sides and came at us with knives and swords and ordered us to give them all our things and the suitcases.

III

As we defended ourselves, we "won" the fight (the fight stopped), and I had stab wounds in my chest and on my back, which by now, thank God, have healed. However, as punishment, they made us give them all our things, even our jackets. Then they let us pass through the forest to the border.

We endured many more *tzuros* [troubles] about which I cannot write in this letter. But with faith in God, who had protected us during the bombing in Warsaw, we smuggled ourselves through the Russian border, and four weeks later found ourselves in the heart of the Russo-Lithuanian border. You can imagine, my beloved ones, it was not easy, yet again, to pass through two borders. We were risking our lives, for here during wartime, if they caught us we would immediately get the death penalty. The Russians here were the same as in Warsaw—and that was the original reason we fled to Lithuania.

Dear Leo had quite a few possessions that he had acquired during the war and needed to sell them before leaving, and that's the reason he told us to leave Warsaw without him and go to Vilna, where we find ourselves now, and that he would follow us as quickly as possible. We are waiting now about five months since then, and he still is not here. I am sure he did not know at the time just how difficult it is to get to here. I have written him a postcard but as yet have not received an answer.

For a few months, we were supported with food by the government, until they learned that Sigmund gave English and French tutoring lessons. Now even this small luxury was withdrawn completely and we do not have the piece of bread to eat that earlier kept us alive. In addition to all the heavy sufferings that we have gone through these past two years, we now face yet another miserable and cruel picture:

IV

Two weeks ago we were sentenced and punished by the Government for smuggling ourselves over the border: (We were given the choice): Either spend 10 months in a concentration camp or pay a fine of 4 dollars per person (that is to say 8 dollars) – which in this currency is 160 *Litai*. When this amount is paid, we would have the right to be readmitted to any city, and would then stand on "free feet."

Beloved and dear Mutti, and beloved sister Eva: Constantly with the thought that we still have, *b"h* (thank God), good and *frum* [pious] parents and siblings, we go again with fresh courage to meet our fate with the awareness that you dear Mutti and beloved Eva, *a.m.v.'s.* [till 120 years], understand the urgency and necessity and know what lies before us, and will, in the fastest way possible get the 8 dollars to us. If not you, my loved ones, who else could help us out of this difficult situation?! Otherwise we are already close to despair, but we have a strong heart to believe in. What is dearer in the world: For parents, is it their children, or for children, is it their parents??? May the *h.b.'h* [God] dismiss our heavy burdens and may the children scattered around the world soon be united in the house of their beloved parents, *a.m.v.'s* [till 120 years].

Today we were by Rosofsky, in 34 Zavalue Street. He said, dear Mama, you should pay him 5 dollars, and we'll get from Frau Rosofsky three times as much (Through the mail I will get 6 *Litai.* and from her 18 *Litai.*). This is for us a higher sum that we immediately have to hand in to the Government. We have one month in which to pay this money. When you give him the money (5 dollars), he should give you a receipt with his signature, and you should send it here immediately by air-mail.

With the awareness that you, dear, precious Mutti will not let our bad luck continue, I wish you, as well as all my other siblings, all good things, and may all the good wishes you bestow on your children be fulfilled. After I receive the receipt from you, which I hope will be here within two weeks, I will send you a detailed letter.

Regards to Jenny, and especially to Julius and Eva. Be greeted and kissed from your

Josef.

MISSING PIECES

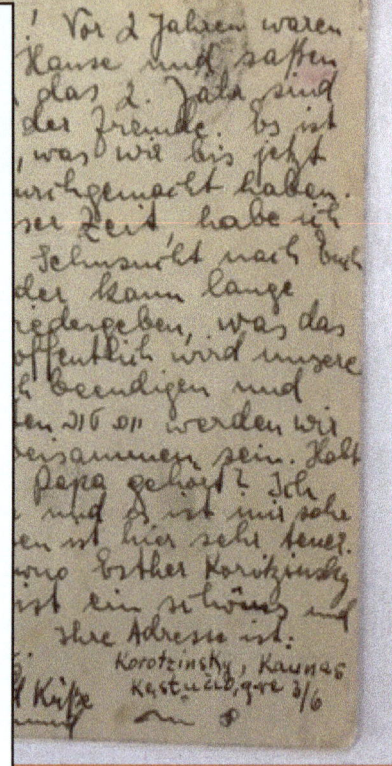

Sigmund to Mutti & siblings
Šiauliai, Lithuania, April 22, 1940

Dear Mutti, and siblings, *amv"sh* [till 120 years],

Unfortunately the Government has deported me to a small city. Josef has remained in Vilna over *Pesach* [Passover]. After *Pesach* he's coming here as well.

My dear ones! Two years ago we were all at home sitting at the Seder. It is now the second year that we're still in a foreign place.

It is very tragic what we all have undergone till now. Now, at this time, I long terribly for all of you. A pen can hardly reproduce what the heart feels. Hopefully, our distress will end soon, and by the next *Yom Tov* [holiday] we will, God willing, all be together.

Have you heard anything from Papa? I am very much alone, and it is very dreary for me. Eating here is very expensive.

I visited Esther Korotzinsky in Kowno [Kaunas]. She is a beautiful and great girl. Her address is: Korotzinsky, Kaunas, Kastucio, g-re 3/6

      A Happy *Pesach*, many greetings and kisses,
                           Sigmund

The last correspondence from Noah Weinreb is displayed on page 66. It is a note written on a small scrap of paper. Responses to Noah's message are written on the reverse side of the note. The reverse side is displayed on page 67. The dates attributed to both the note and the responses are estimates.

The salutation on the note indicates that the recipient was Ella's mother, Rachel Rottenberg, who had remained in nearby Berlin. The note is signed "Noach," which was Noah's Hebrew name.

It is probable that the note was smuggled out of the Sachsenhausen concentration camp. While the response was never delivered, the handwriting on the back suggests that more than one person added to the message.

Although it is not clear how the note reached Eva in Portugal, it remained in her possession.

MISSING PIECES

Front of fragment:

Date estimate: ca. May 1, 1940

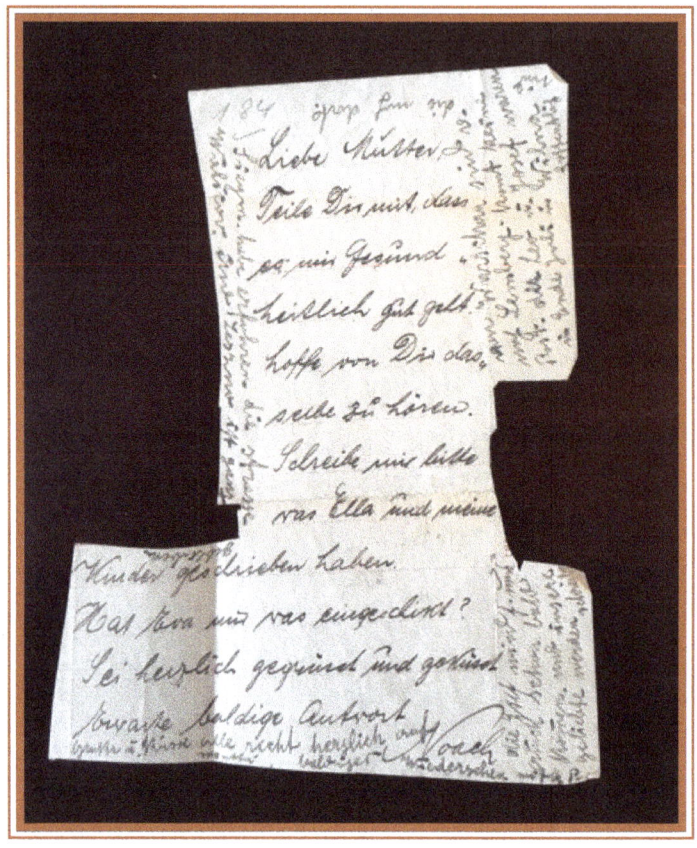

Dear Mother, (Mother-in-Law Rachel Rottenberg)

I share with you that regarding my health all is good. I hope to hear the same from you. Please write to me what Ella and my children wrote to you. Did Eva include anything for me? Heartfelt greetings and kisses. I await an early reply,

Noach [Hebrew name]

Around the edges: (added in response)

The time will soon come and our loved ones will write from Warsaw. From Lemberg (Lvov, Ukraine) there is no mail. Leo and Josef were in Vilna at the end of July (1940). Hopefully they are still there. I heard the street Sigmund is on is Walicov.

A FAMILY STORY RETOLD

Back of fragment:

Date estimate: after July, 1940

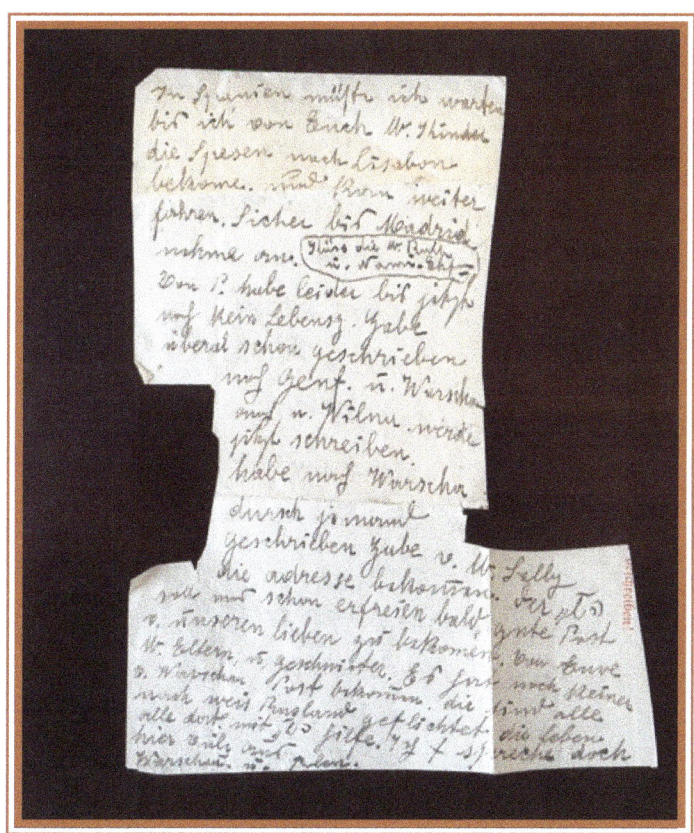

I had to wait in Spain until I received from you, dear children, the money to get to Lisbon and from there I can travel on at least till Madrid. [Ella was en route from Mikolc, Hungary to join Eva and Julius in Lisbon, Portugal]. **About P. (Papa) unfortunately I have till now no signs of life.**

On advice I wrote to Warsaw, and I'll write now to Vilna. Through someone who gave me the address, I wrote to Warsaw. May *Hashem* [God] grant that we receive good news soon from our loved ones – from your dear parents and your brethren. I have still have no posts from Warsaw, they all fled to new Russia. They are all there, with God's help. I speak of Warsaw and Poland.

***Bottom*:**

Heartfelt greetings and kisses to all, hopefully we'll soon see each other again, Kisses to Rutti [Ruthie] and Nami [Naomi]　　　　**Mutti**

Jeny (Ella's sister) to niece Eva
Charlottenburg, Berlin, July 14, 1940

My very dear Eva,

As I see from the postcard, you have been informed of the tragedy that has befallen all of us, the death of your beloved, dear Papa. I am deeply shocked by this inevitable fact.

It happened on the 3rd of May, it was on a Friday, I did not hear about it until about three weeks later.

The Margulies family intercepted the telegram and gave it secretly to me so that at least dear Oma [Rachel Rottenberg] would not know about it.

She's always asking, again and again, why is there no mail, but till now we could always make an excuse — she would not, God forbid, be able to withstand it. [When I found out], the telephone dropped out of my hand.

Dear *Evschen*! We have to comfort ourselves due to this heavy and bitter blow to all of us. God has given, God has taken away. The wound remains. Hopefully your dear Mother won't learn about it too quickly.

The Entry Papers (Ella's) came to the Portuguese Consul about the end of June—they were in transit at least four months. I received mail from Jenny (Weinreb, Eva's sister) dated February 14th, and a postcard to Oma [R. Rottenberg] from Mutti (Ella) that was written in January, according to the stamp on the postcard. 4 to 5 months is usual for ordinary mail, compared to Air Mail which at most takes 8 days, sometimes even 4 to 5 days.

I was unable to pass along this information to the boys. Someone had already been instructed to tell the children in Lithuania. The burial will, of course, be in the Community Cemetery *(Adas Yisroel,* Berlin*)*.

The flight ticket should have been here by now. I have been there several times and I couldn't get it back. I have to go there again because it is being held by an aide of the Consul.

Uncle Siggi is worried because he's written to you twice and has not received any answer, he is worried as well about Klara and the children. From whom did you receive the news? Did the Palestine-Office (Zionist group) write you or was it the *Hilfsverein* [German Jewish Relief Agency]?

Dear Oma is weak, she has problems with her feet. Well, dear Evchen! Be strong, it was God's will and there's nothing any of us can do about it.

Your children are pure dolls. May you have much good fortune and joy from them, so that they will lighten the burden of this heavy tragedy. Have you told Jenny?

When Bali writes, then Klara can add a few lines so that I can tell Uncle Sigmund. Lastly, Bali does not need to know, he'll find out soon enough. Remain warmly greeted and kissed, as well as your dear Julius and Jenny. You cannot give my regards to Mutti (Ella) from me, she would want to read this letter, hopefully she does not yet know about it.

Your sad Aunt Jeny

Warm greetings and kisses, **Josi**

Warm greetings and kisses, **Toska**

MISSING PIECES

Josef to grandmother Rachel
Kuršėnai, Lithuania, September 10, 1940

Dear Oma,

We have received your lovely card with joy, and share with you that we are, thank God, healthy.

All refugees from Poland have been sent into villages and we are among them.

I play the accordion and piano here in an orchestra and earn so I can get along. Siegmund also earns. How is it going with you, Dear Oma? Are you healthy? How is the Margulies family? And Fluss?

Be very much greeted and kissed by your grandsons,

Josef and Sigmund.

Sigmund to grandmother Rachel
Kuršėnai, Lithuania, November 15, 1940

Dear Grandmother (very formal),

We've just received a letter from dear Mutti and it made us very happy. I have, thank God, work, and I earn for me and for Josef. How are you? Hopefully we'll soon see each other again.

Also, Martha and the brothers (Leslie and Benno, in London) thank God, are doing well. My brother Leo has married in Warsaw. Write to us soon again. How is Aunt Jeny (Jeny Fluss)?

Be kissed from your **Sigmund.**

Strong heartfelt greetings, **Josef**

Sigmund to Mutti (Ella) and siblings
Kuršėnai, Lithuania, November 14, 1940

Dear Mutti and Siblings! Till 120 yrs.

Yesterday, Josef came back from the Schawels, where we had lived before, and brought back the card and the letter. Unfortunately we had to move because we were not allowed to live in the big city any longer. Here this is a small city with a 2,000 inhabitants.

I'm working in a sugar factory and earn enough for Josef and me to eat, but not enough to buy any clothes. I work from 11:00 at night till 7:00 in the morning and sleep during the day. I hope you received our last letter.

Things are all right with us as far as our health, but we still cannot grasp the loss of our dear Papa. For us it will remain a deep wound forever; but what can we attempt against God's hand.

Life is now very hard and a very critical time is upon us. But hopefully the hour will yet come in which we and you, dear Mother and Siblings, will see each other again. I really love you so much, dear Mutti, and you cannot imagine how much I miss you all. Dear Mutti, you write something about Montevideo and I did not understand any of it. In case you could create papers for us then we could emigrate from here. All the consulates are no longer in Kowno, they are all now in Moscow.

It is very surprising that Leo has written to you with no return address. We will write to him. You can write him at the following address: Leo Weinreb c/o Freiman, Warsaw, Wolguska 7 m. 33 I'm also pleased that things are, thank God, good with Martha and Siblings [in London]. Write again soon and perhaps you can send us a small package of warm underwear. Take note of our new address: S. Weinreb c/o Resnik, Kursenai, Dariaus Gerena 2, Lithuania Stay healthy and many kisses, always thinking of you,

Sigmund

Mali (Ella's sister) & daughters to Ella
London, England, ca. September, 1940

My dear beloved Sister, *AMV"SH* [till 120]

It is shortly before *Yomtov* [Holiday], so I want to write you, my dear Sister, a few lines and wishes. Yes, it's unfortunate we're so torn apart from each other, only these letters keep us together. The world is so big, but the *tzures* [woes] are even bigger.

God in heaven should have mercy on all of us and help us all, still in this lifetime, to be able to see, hear and write (to each other). I'm very happy you and your dear children are together, and dear God will help you to enjoy much *naches* [pride] from them. *Omen* [Amen]!

Have you heard anything at all from our dear loved ones at home? We are completely cut off, we've had no Posts from anyone. We also want to move from here to Paris, dear children, but because of the bad conditions we have to wait.

God should have mercy, one hopes and says *tehillim* [Psalms] that the *yeshua* [salvation] should come soon. My dear sister, I wish you a happy, healthy New Year, you should stay healthy and strong and all your wishes should be fulfilled. *Omen* [Amen]!

Heartfelt greetings and kisses from your always-thinking-of-you Sister, **Mali**

Best greetings and wishes Good *Yomtov* to all, **Markus**

A FAMILY STORY RETOLD

My dear, precious Aunty Ella (till 120)

Things are, b"h [Thank God], going well for us. I hope to hear the same from you. We live very near to dear Mutti and Papa.

I wish everything good to you. And a good New Year. Dear God should help that we shall, in joy, see each other again. Omen.

Many greetings and kisses to Julius, Eva, Jenny and the two very sweet dolls.

Paula

Dear Aunt Ella, till 120,

I wish you everything good for the New Year. How are things going with you? Everything b"h is going well for us.

Next time more. Many greetings and kisses, also, greetings from me to Julius, Eva and Jenny.

Susi

Dear Eva, Julius and loved little children (till 120)

I wish you all a happy, healthy New Year! The yeshua should come soon for us and for all the family. We certainly hope the New Year will bring our salvation, and it should only be that our dear loved ones in the K.L. (*Konzentration Lager* — concentration camp) be freed by this hand. We are sitting here and wait hour after hour for this help.

Be all of you greeted and kissed from your

Tante [aunt] **Mali**

Josef (age 18) to sister Eva & Julius in Lisbon
Kuršėnai, Lithuania, May 8, 1941

My dear ones, till 120 yrs.,

We received your letter of April 18th, and we're happy to hear something from you again. Surely you have already received the news that Sigmund had married. *Mazel Tov* to you all. He is, thank God, very well settled in and is very blessed with his wife.

Dear *Mamaleben* ["Mommy"], I have not yet received the little package with coffee. Hopefully it will still come. I have inquired at the Post Office about the sending of clothing here. I was told you can send whatever and how much you want, but the items may not be totally new.

So I ask you to be careful for me. First, 1 pair shoes 44-45, and 2 shirts size 38-39, sent Express, you can include 1/4 or 1/2 dozen *skarpetten* [?]; those one can get here, and they are very cheap! You understand me.

When I get that package I'll be very happy and will forever be grateful to you. You have written me that you have suits for both of us. For Sigmund it is not very urgent since he has 2 or 3 suits, but for me it is of great importance that you to send me one suit. After I get this package I'll give you my measurements because you're probably wondering how big I am: 1.86 meters. I am also, thank God, broad-shouldered. My dear ones, I'm playing the accordion and piano in an orchestra and it is going very well for me except that which I've written to you. All the money I earn goes to support my livelihood and therefore it's impossible for me to acquire clothing.

NB: If I wouldn't eat for 3 months then I'd be able to buy a pair of simple shoes. You understand how it is? One may not sin, one must trust in God, then all will be good. We have become very popular through our skills. Sigmund conducts a choir that is greatly admired and I am a leader of a 6-man brass band. Other than that I play accompaniment for ballet lessons and I'm asked to play at dances in Siauliai and in Kowno (Lithuania). I've even been photographed for the newspaper as a good bandleader. I'll send you the article about it. Our greatest wish is that you, dear Mama, get healthy, and all of us will again be helped. Be well and strong.

From **Josef.**

Please pay close and exact attention to my letter, and take care of it quickly, the faster you send the package the better, I'm so sure of it.

A FAMILY STORY RETOLD

Photograph in the authors' private collection

MISSING PIECES

Sigmund (Age 20) to Mutti & siblings
Kuršėnai, Lithuania, May 15, 1941

Photograph in the authors' private collection

Dear Mutti and dear Siblings, till 120 yrs.

It is my greatest joy and good fortune to announce to you that I have, with *Mazel*, [good fortune] gotten married. You cannot even imagine how quickly and unanticipated this was, but I had to quickly grab this good luck with both hands.

We had a small *chuppah* [wedding under a canopy] in another city, since nowadays one cannot have any showing of religious ceremonies here, and we try to conduct ourselves very modestly. Dear Mutti, you have acquired a daughter-in-law whose characteristics are exactly like yours. She is a very energetic, heart-cultured and warm person.

My wish to you is that you enjoy only *naches* [pride] from us and hear only about *simches* [happy events] from us. **It is a great pity our dear Father was no longer fated to hear any *b'soros tovos* [good news] about his sons.**

I cried a lot under the *chuppah,* but the Lord consoled me and conveyed to me that for us a time will still come when we will see each other again, drink a *L'chaim* [to life] to our well-being—we have actually done this—that all good things we wish upon ourselves should be fulfilled.

I have, *B"H* [thank God], a good job as chief cashier in a Cooperative. My dear wife works as a cashier in another government business. Josef will probably also get a job soon. He is staying with us, but temporarily still sleeps there, where he had been sleeping. Here we have 2 little rooms, but we're very glad to have them, because at this time one has to be very unpretentious…

Hopefully your foot problems are over and you are able to go out. How's it going with you, dear *Jennylein*? Please send me a photo of yourself. I'm including 2 photos in this letter. Please do not include any written replies with them, since the Post no longer accepts them.

Greetings and kisses to you all, Your **Sigmund**

Heartfelt greetings from **Josef**

(Toibe, Sigmund's new wife added these lines in Yiddish)

To my dear Mother-in-law:

Dear Mother, I'm adding to the greetings from your noble and fine son Sigmund. I understand what an intelligent, fine woman you are for having raised such a fine son.

I hope to earn your love and belief in me, your newly acquired daughter. I hope we'll see each other soon and we'll be able to get to know each other. And then I hope you will like me.

Now, from far away, Your daughter,

Toibe

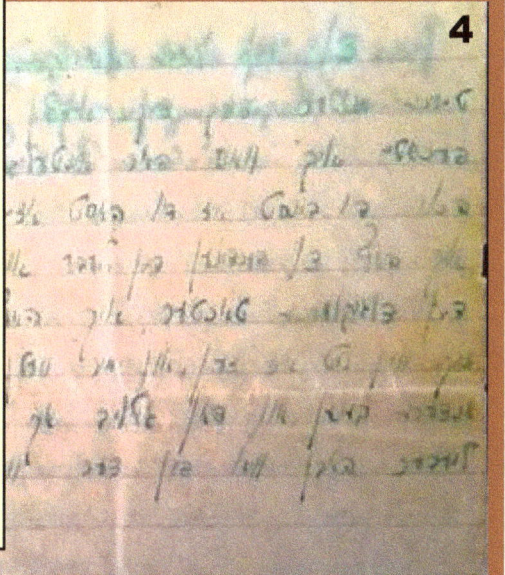

MISSING PIECES

Sigmund to Mutti & siblings
Kuršėnai, Lithuania, (No date) ca. June, 1941

This is the last letter received from Sigmund and Josef.

Dear Mutti and Sister & Brother-in-Law

A half our ago Josef brought your letter which I enjoyed very much. I hope by now you have received the letter I sent to you. It is almost 12 o'clock, and I finished work not long ago. My "TEIBELE"—that's my wife's name—is already asleep. She worked today and is certainly tired. Dear Mutti, you cannot imagine how I, newly married, feel. I have become much more self-powerful and thoughtful and that is good for me.

Unfortunately, it was not ordained for our beloved Father to hear good news from his sons. On our beloved Father's Yahrzeit I expressed the wish that dear God will console us over the loss of our beloved father and save us from all bad things in the future. May dear God grant us to have the one pleasure of seeing each other and being together, and that you, dear Mutti, should live to experience joy from us.

After a long time, I finally hear something about our siblings in England (in the letter from Mutti to which, apparently, he is responding). I'm very happy that all are healthy and well over there. Only it surprises me that Eva did not add any lines. Dear Eva, please add a few details, otherwise one immediately worries.

Things are, thank God, going well for me, and I'm very satisfied with my work. Though I work 13 hours a day, I'm happy that at least I have a job. Josef unfortunately is not good yet with Lithuanian, but eventually, with time, he'll learn it.

Yes, dear Mutti, the Gymnasium [high school] brought me many benefits, which I can only now appreciate, as you so strongly emphasized the value of my learning at the time. I speak good Russian and Lithuanian, and even peruse books in Lithuanian at my job.

In a short while we'll be getting Russian passes, and in September we'll probably have to serve [in the Russian army]. **But, dear Mutti, do not compare the Russian Military duty to the Germans. In the Russian Military they educate you, and one comes back from the Service very satisfied. When I appeared for the inspection they already told me where I'll be serving. Based on my education I was chosen to be a translator and communicator at the Telefunken Station. Here, facility with languages is very exceptional and is sought after in the Military. Besides that I will be given a position as choir conductor, as I conduct a chorus here. It will certainly be good there. My wife will receive my salary, and everyone will be taken care of.**

Josef earns a little, and at least has something. Otherwise there is nothing new. I'm very happy, dear Mutti, that your foot is better. What are you doing, Dear Jenny? You must be a big girl by now. I've asked you so often – dear *Jennylein,* to send me a photo. I ask urgently that next time you don't forget.

How are your little girls, dear Eva? All to whom I've shown their picture cannot believe they are children; they all say these are dolls. How are you, dear Julius? Are you still working at your old business? Please also add a few words, I'd really like that. It is almost 1 (a.m), and I have to be at work early. To all, heartfelt greetings and kisses from your loving son and brother, **Sigmund**

My dear ones, Thank you for your letter, which we greatly enjoyed. I wish you all good things, only health, and don't think that we have nothing to eat, since healthwise we're all good. Thank God things are good, only I ask you to immediately send the shoes and suits, wear them out a bit (so they won't seem new) so I won't have any difficulties (with customs). Otherwise all is in order, only we should all be healthy. From your **Josef**

Unfortunately, now one cannot send anymore by Air Mail, just ordinary Post.

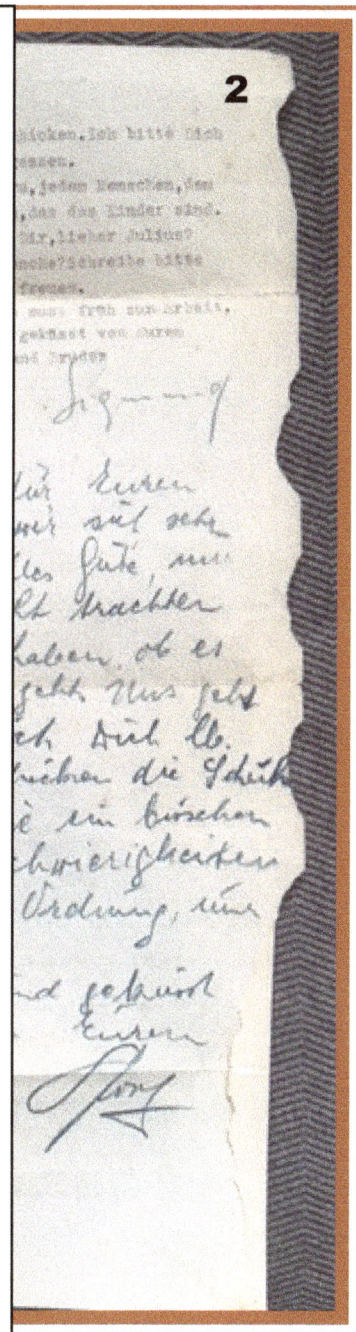

The timing and cessation of correspondence suggest that Sigmund, Toibe and Josef were murdered in or around Kursenai in the summer of 1941. (See pages 29, 31)

MISSING PIECES

Izydor (Eva's brother-in-law) to Ella in Lisbon
Warsaw Ghetto, Poland, October 26, 1941

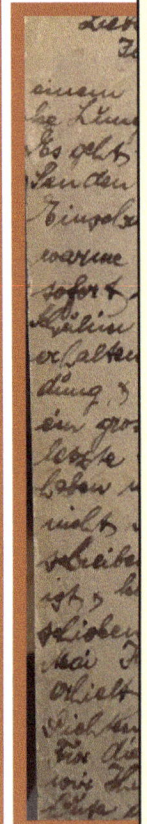
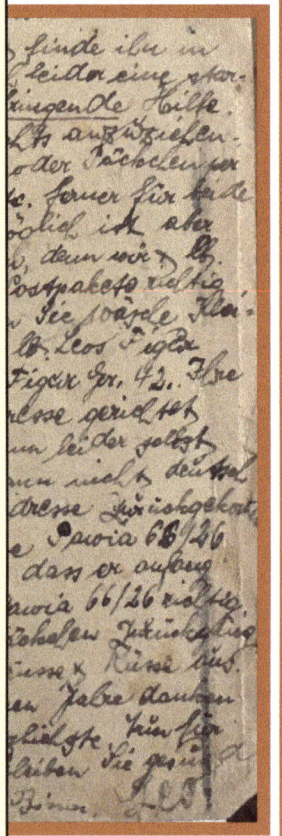

Dear Family Weinreb:

I am at the moment with Leo and his dear wife and find him very ill. He has a very serious lung infection and urgently needs help. Winter is coming soon and they unfortunately have nothing to draw on. Therefore, please continue to send him packages or parcels containing tea, coffee, cocoa, oil sardines etc. Also, for both, warm underwear, clothing etc., whatever you can, but send it immediately. Packages that were sent to us about 14 days ago are just now arriving. 5 kilogram packages are the easiest to receive here. Dear Leo's wife's name is Bina Weinreb. When you send underwear and clothing for both of them, you should know dear Leo's figure: a tall slim man; she seems a slim figure, about size 42.

Your last cards from September 29, '41, and October 2, '41 for Leo that were sent to our address were received on November 20, and have been given to Leo. Unfortunately he cannot write by himself because he is so ill, and his wife cannot write in German. It surprises me that one package to Leo's address was returned. You can, with confidence, send things to their address: **Pawia 66/26**. Incidentally, I just heard from him that in early May he received your card from April 17, '41 at the Pawia 66/26 address. So I cannot imagine why the package was returned.

Please give dear Julius and Eva all greetings and kisses. All the best is wished for a heartfelt cure today. Greetings from the heart, stay healthy and send something to Leo immediately.

Your **Isi,** (added, names only) **Bina / Leo**

A FAMILY STORY RETOLD

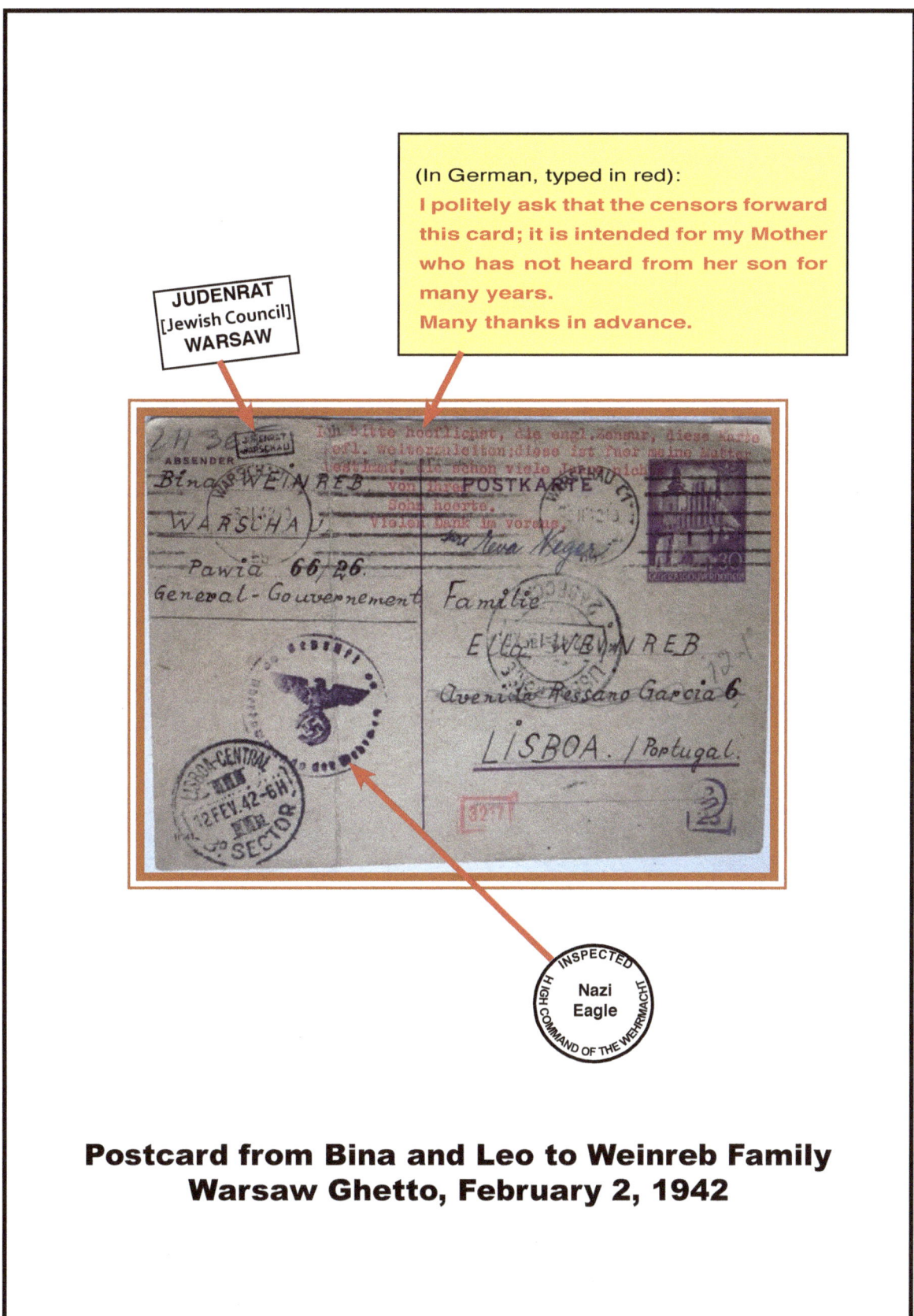

**Postcard from Bina and Leo to Weinreb Family
Warsaw Ghetto, February 2, 1942**

Leo to sister Eva in Lisbon
Warsaw Ghetto, April 21, 1942

My dear ones,

I was happy to receive your card in package Number 3. I sincerely thank you for all you do for me. Were it not for your packages I wouldn't know what I would do, since life circumstances are very difficult. With thanks, I received from Mama the 5 kilo package of sardines with a pair of ladies socks.

Why are there no messages from dear Mama? I hope that I will still receive the 10 kilo package. Please, when you send me anything, put it in a small package; it comes here faster and I need the help soon.

My wife will, with God's help, soon be lying in. Kisses to Mama. Greetings and kisses,

Your **Leo** and **Bina**

A FAMILY STORY RETOLD

... July 6, 1942

My Dear Ones! Dear Sister!

I am delighted to have received your letters. I thank you very much for the caring you demonstrate for your brother. I have still not received any news from dear Mama and don't know where I can write to her.

News that I'm happy to share with you is that my wife has given birth to a daughter, and I have named her Rachel. When you get this card it will have been about 5 weeks since. How are your dear children? Are they healthy?

How is dear Julius? How is business? I'm earning absolutely nothing and rely on your support, about which, since two weeks now, I have heard nothing.

I have read the card from Josy [Josef] and thank you for it. Why don't you use my address? I await news from you as soon as possible. Best wishes and kisses together with Wife and Daughter,

Your **Leo**

This is the last correspondence from Leo.

MISSING PIECES

EPILOGUE

The Museum of Jewish Heritage – A Living Memorial to the Holocaust
New York City, 2020

In a room filled with artifacts describing Operation Barbarossa and the beginning of mass murder, there are two small, lead *dreidels* (four-sided children's tops traditionally associated with the Hanukkah holiday).[28] The *dreidels* were gifted to the Museum by *Yahad–In Unum* (Hebrew and Latin, meaning "Together–in One"), the organization founded by Father Patrick Desbois.[29]

Yahad–In Unum is dedicated to identifying the thousands of mass graves in the German-occupied former Soviet Union, a region where millions of Jews once lived.[29] The *dreidels* are not simply remains. They are the valued belongings of someone who once lived and is now buried with countless others in an unmarked and once forgotten grave. Each of them had hopes, dreams, family, and a life story.

When the tattered brown envelope stuffed with correspondence was discovered behind the couch not so long ago, we knew that it was important to give voice to the writers by sharing their stories, thus bringing us closer to saying, "We found you."

BG

MISSING PIECES

Annotations & Endnotes

1. The authors have cited documentation from the *Memorial Book – Victims of the Persecution of Jews under the National Socialist Tyranny in Germany 1933-1945* located in the German Federal Archives (*Das Bundesarchiv*) when referencing the date, fate, and place of death of family members murdered during the Nazi reign of terror and the Holocaust. In the absence of this information, as is the case with Sigmund and Josef, testimony reported by family members to the Central Data Base of Shoah Victims' names at Yad Vashem has been used to augment and verify details provided in the correspondence. https://www.bundesarchiv.de/gedenkbuch. Accessed March-July, 2020. (The website address was updated 11/2020.)

2. The *Irgun Ze'vai Le'umi* ("*Etzel*") was the National Military Organization founded in Palestine in 1931 by a group of Haganah commanders. Primary goals included military training, the procurement of arms, and immigration of endangered Jews from Eastern Europe to Palestine, despite stringent quotas imposed by the British. The Irgun later became part of Israel's Haganah.

Brzezinski, Matthew. *Isaac's Army: A Story of Courage and Survival in Nazi-Occupied Poland.*, Random House, 2012.

Jewish Virtual Library. "Irgun: The Altalena Affair." https://www.jewishvirtuallibrary.org/the-altalena-affair. Accessed July 3, 2020.

Jewish Virtual Library. "Background and Overview of the Irgun." https://www.jewishvirtuallibrary.org/background-and-overview-of-the-irgun-etzel. Accessed June 11, 2020.

Rubin, Gil S. "Was Polish Anti-Semitism Actually Zionism?" Tablet Magazine. Oct 14, 2015. https://www.tabletmag.com/sections/arts-letters/articles/polish-anti-semitism-zionism. Accessed May 1, 2020.

3. Yad Vashem. "Warsaw ghetto uprising." https://www.yadvashem.org/holocaust/about/combat-resistance/warsaw-ghetto.html. Accessed July 3, 2020.

4 Jewish Virtual Library. "The Nuremberg Laws: The Reich Citizenship Law." https://www.jewishvirtuallibrary.org/the-reich-citizenship-law. Accessed December 17, 2020.

United States Holocaust Memorial Museum. "The Nuremberg Laws: The Reich Citizenship Law: First Regulation." Holocaust Encyclopedia. https://encyclopedia.ushmm.org/content/en/article/nuremberg-laws. Accessed on December 17, 2020.

See also: extensive resources at The Weiner Holocaust Library. wienerlibrary.co.uk.

5. Jewish Museum Berlin. "Polenaktion ("Polish Action," 1938). https://www.jmberlin.de/en/topic-polenaktion-1938. Accessed November 17, 2020.

6. In the official (Nazi) deportation list, Sascha is identified as Sarah Leanda Sascha. The names of Jewish females were changed by the Nazis to "Sarah" to identify them as Jews.

7. German Federal Archives (*Das Bundesarchiv*). *Memorial Book – Victims of the Persecution of Jews under the National Socialist Tyranny in Germany 1933-1945* "The Expulsion of Polish Jews from the German Reich 1938/1939 and their records." https://www.bundesarchiv.de/gedenkbuch. Accessed Jun 15, 2020.
(See also: https://www.bundesarchiv.de/gedenkbuch/introduction/#expulsion)

Harris, Bonnie M. "From German Jews to Polish Refugees: Germany's Polenaktion and the Zbaszyn Deportations of October 1938. ResearchGate. https://www.researchgate.net/publication/327592691_From_German_Jews_to_Polish_Refugees_Germany%27s_Polenaktion_and_the_Zbaszyn_Deportations_of_October_1938. Accessed November 30, 2020.

Jewish Museum Berlin. "We were being driven like hunted animals." https://www.jmberlin.de/en/max-karp-polenaktion. Accessed December 14, 2020

Jewish Museum Frankfurt. "Victim of the 'Polenaktion' in 1938." https://www.juedischesmuseum.de/en/explore/documents-and-photos/detail/polenaktion-1938/. Accessed November 30, 2020.

8. Nazi Germany annexed Austria into the greater German Reich in March 1938. Adolf Hitler was born in Austria, making its inclusion in the greater German Reich particularly meaningful to him. History: "Germany Annexes Austria." https://www.history.com/this-day-in-history/germany-annexes-austria. Accessed May 20, 2020.

9. Auschwitz III-Monowitz was established to provide forced labor for I.G. Farben, a producer of chemicals, most notably Zyklon-B pesticide used in the gas chambers at Auschwitz and elsewhere to murder Jews and other identified "enemies" of the Reich.

Dwork, Deborah and van Pelt, Robert. *Auschwitz*. W.W. Norton & Co., pp. 197-335.

van Pelt, Robert Jan with Greenbaum, Miriam and Ferreiro, Luis (Eds.). "A German Concentration Camp in Auschwitz," *Auschwitz–Not Long Ago, Not Far Away* (Exhibition Catalogue), Abbeville Publishers, pp. 87-109.

10. Weinreich, Max. *Hitler's Professors* (Second Ed.). Yale University Press, pp. 5-83.

11. Betar was an activist Zionist youth movement founded by Vladmir Jabotinsky in 1923, in Riga, Latvia. The organization was dedicated to *aliyah* (immigration to Palestine) and the creation of an independent Jewish State. During the 1930s, the group was concerned with immigration to Palestine by any means necessary. Affiliations included the New Zionist Organization, the National Labor Federation, and *Irgun Ze'vai Le'umi* in Palestine. https://www.jewishvirtuallibrary.org/betar https://yivoencyclopedia.org/article.aspx/Betar.

Kadosh, Sara. "Youth Aliyah Policies and the rescue of Jewish Children from Europe 1939-1942." *Proceedings of the World Congress of Jewish Studies*, 1997, V. 12, p. 95.

Melzer, Emanuel. "Betar." YIVO Encyclopedia of Jews in Eastern Europe 8 August 20. https://yivoencyclopedia.org/article.aspx/Betar. Accessed July 18, 2020.

12. JewishGen. "A Timeline of the Holocaust (1939-1945)." https://www.jewishgen.org/ForgottenCamps/General/TimeEng.html. Accessed on June 1, 2020.

United States Holocaust Memorial Museum. "Timeline of Events: 1933-1938. Holocaust Encyclopedia. https://www.ushmm.org/learn/timeline-of-events/1933-1938. "Accessed on June 1, 2020.

The Weiner Holocaust Library. "The Holocaust Explained." https://www.theholocaustexplained.org/events-in-the-history-of-the-holocaust-1933-to-1939/. Accessed on June 22, 2020.

13. United States Holocaust Memorial Museum. "Invasion of the Soviet Union, June 1941." Holocaust Encyclopedia. https://encyclopedia.ushmm.org/content/en/article/invasion-of-the-soviet-union-june-1941. Accessed on December 16, 2020.

14. United States Holocaust Memorial Museum. "Einsatzgruppen: An Overview." Holocaust Encyclopedia. https://encyclopedia.ushmm.org/content/en/article/einsatzgruppen. Accessed on June 15, 2020.

Desbois, Patrick. T*he Holocaust by Bullets: A Priest's Journey to Uncover the Truth Behind the Murder of 1.5 Million Jews*, St. Martins Griffin, 2008.

Facing History and Ourselves. "The Holocaust in Lithuania." https://www.facinghistory.org/resource-library/resistance-during-holocaust/holocaust-lithuania. Accessed December 13, 2020.

15. Weinreb, Lazarus Leslie. *One Boy of Ten: The Life and Times of Lazarus Leslie Weinreb*, Docostory Ltd. 2005, p. 24.

16. German Federal Archives (*Das Bundesarchiv*). Memorial Book–Victims of the Persecution of Jews under the National Socialist Tyranny in Germany. "The Expulsion of Polish Jews from the German Reich 1938/1939 and their records." https://www.bundesarchiv.de/gedenkbuch/ Accessed Jun 15, 2020.

17. Yad Vashem. The Central Database of Shoah Victims' Names. "Alter Albert Meyer Isaak." https://yvng.yadvashem.org/nameDetails.html?language=en&itemid=11527851&ind=1. Accessed July 3, 2020.

18. United States Holocaust Memorial Museum. "Invasion of the Soviet Union, June 1941." https://encyclopedia.ushmm.org/content/en/article/invasion-of-the-soviet-union-june-1941. Accessed December 1, 2020.

Desbois, Patrick. T*he Holocaust by Bullets: A Priest's Journey to Uncover the Truth Behind the Murder of 1.5 Million Jews*, St. Martins Griffin, 2008.

United States Holocaust Memorial Museum. "Einsatzgruppen: An Overview." Holocaust Encyclopedia. https://encyclopedia.ushmm.org/content/en/article/einsatzgruppen. Accessed on July 21, 2020.

Vanagaite, Ruta and Zuroff, Efraim. *Our People: Discovering Lithuania's Hidden Holocaust*. Roman & Littlefield, 2016.

Yad Vashem. Einsatzgruppen. https://www.yadvashem.org/untoldstories/documents/GenBack/Einsatzgruppen.pdf. Accessed on December 1, 2020.

19. Beit Hatfutsot. "Kursenai." https://dbs.anumuseum.org.il/skn/en/c6/e208400/Place/Kursenai. Accessed on December 1, 2020.

Rosin, Joseph. *Protecting our Litvak Heritage: A History of 50 Jewish Communities in Lithuania*, 108. https://www.jewishgen.org/yizkor/ybip/YBIP_Lithuania3.html. Accessed on June 15, 2020.

20. Rosin, Joseph. *Protecting our Litvak Heritage: A History of 50 Jewish Communities in Lithuania*, 108. https://www.jewishgen.org/yizkor/ybip/YBIP_Lithuania3.html. Accessed on June 15, 2020. Photos used with permission.

JewishGen. "Kursenai (Kurshan)." https://www.jewishgen.org/yizkor/lithuania6/lit6_108.html. Accessed on June 26, 2020.

Yahad-In Unum. "Kuršėnai." The Map of Evidence: Holocaust by Bullets. https://yahadmap.org/#village/kur-nai-kurshan-kurshany-iauliai-lithuania.684. Accessed on December 12, 2020.

21. The *Irgun Ze'vai Le'umi* ("*Etzel*") was the National Military Organization founded in Palestine in 1931 by a group of Haganah commanders. Primary goals included military training, the procurement of arms, and immigration of endangered Jews from Eastern Europe to Palestine, despite stringent British quotas. The Irgun later became part of Israel's Haganah. (See additional references, endnote number 2, p. 87).

22. The following volumes provide an excellent account of the Warsaw ghetto and the ghetto uprising. They include writings by ghetto residents that were preserved in the buried ghetto archive (code name: *Oyneg Shabes*) as well as a detailed description of the resistance groups that participated in the uprising.

Kassow, Samuel, D. *Who will write our history? Rediscovering a Hidden Archive from the Warsaw Ghetto.* Vintage Books, 2007, pp. 333-388.

Museum of Jewish Heritage-A Living Memorial to the Holocaust. *Scream The Truth At The World: Emanuel Ringelblum and the Hidden Archive of the Warsaw Ghetto* (Exhibition Catalogue), 2001, p. 91

Roskies, David G. *Voices from the Warsaw Ghetto: Writing Our History.* Yale University Press, 2019.

23. United States Holocaust Memorial Museum. "Deportations to and from the Warsaw ghetto." Holocaust Encyclopedia. https://encyclopedia.ushmm.org/content/en/article/deportations-to-and-from-the-warsaw-ghetto. Accessed on June 10, 2020.

24. Gerson, Beth & Isaak, M. David, (Eds.). *Our Story: Martha & Pinkas Isaak* (Rev. ed.), GERISA INC, (2020).

25. Ibid.

26. Lieberman, Jenny (Wilzig). *Jenny's Journey: The Life Story of Jenny (Wilzig) Lieberman*, Docustory Publishing House, 2003.

27. The *Irgun Ze'vai Le'umi* ("*Etzel*") was the National Military Organization founded in Palestine in 1931 by a group of Haganah commanders. Primary goals included military training, the procurement of arms, and immigration of endangered Jews from Eastern Europe to Palestine, despite stringent quotas imposed by the British. The Irgun later became part of Israel's Haganah. (See additional references, endnote number 2, p. 87).

28. The Museum of Jewish Heritage - A Living Memorial to the Holocaust. "The Beginning of the Holocaust," *Auschwitz – Not Long Ago, Not Far Away* (Musealia).

29. YIVO Institute for Jewish Research. "Memory of a Past and the Battle for a Promising Future." https://yivo.org/Father-Desbois. (Presentation) Accessed on June 20, 2020.

Bauer, Yehuda. *A History of the Holocaust* (Rev. ed.). Franklin Watts. 2001, p. 215.

Rosenbaum, Alan. "The unknown Holocaust in the former Soviet Union." The Jerusalem Post. December 21, 2019. https://www.jpost.com/israel-news/holocaust-remembrance-in-the-occupied-ussr-611440. Accessed July 3, 2020.

van Pelt, Robert Jan with Greenbaum, Miriam and Ferreiro, Luis (Eds.). "The Beginning of the Holocaust." *Auschwitz–Not Long Ago, Not Far Away* (Exhibition Catalogue), Abbeville Publishers, p. 117.

Yad Vashem. "Soviet Union." https://www.yadvashem.org/untoldstories/documents/GenBack/Soviet_Union.pdf. Accessed July 3, 2020.

M. DAVID ISAAK & BETH GERSON

The authors are gallery educators at the Museum of Jewish Heritage—A Living Memorial to the Holocaust, in New York, NY. M. David Isaak is the grandson and nephew of the writers whose letters and postcards are included in this volume.

Related publications include

Our Story: Martha & Pinkas Isaak, 2011; Revised edition, 2020.

https://www.gerisabooks.org

www.ingramcontent.com/pod-product-compliance
Lightning Source LLC
Chambersburg PA
CBHW042027100526
44587CB00029B/4328